DANCING
TO
PLAY OR TO PRAY

A Comparative Study of Prahlāda Yakshagānam in Kūchipūdi and Mélattūr Bhāgavata Méla Traditions

DANCING TO PLAY OR TO PRAY

A Comparative Study of Prahlāda Yakshagānam in Kūchipūdi and Mélattūr Bhāgavata Méla Traditions

Dr. Munagapati Samba Siva Raju

KANISHKA PUBLISHERS, DISTRIBUTORS
NEW DELHI-110 002

KANISHKA PUBLISHERS, DISTRIBUTORS
4697/5-21 A, Ansari Road, Daryaganj
New Delhi-110 002
Phones : 2327 0497, 2328 8285
Fax : 011-2328 8285
E-mail: kanishka_publishing@yahoo.co.in

Dancing to Play or to Pray

First Published 2010

ISBN 978-81-8457-221-6

PRINTED IN INDIA

Published by Madan Sachdeva for Kanishka Publishers, Distributors, 4697/5-21A, Ansari Road, Daryaganj, New Delhi-110 002, Typeset by Sunshine Graphics, Delhi, and Printed at Rajdhani Printers, Delhi.

Foreword

In the contemporary Indian classical dance we hardly find any comparative study of dance forms. Therefore, the present study by Dr. M.S. Siva Raju is really a very refreshing one. His study is a pioneering attempt to look into the roots of two South Indian dance forms through a critical and methodological analysis. This study is also important in another sense. His study is based on rigorous fieldwork and extensive interviews with eminent scholars/performers in the concerned area of research. It is rooted in rich empirical data.

This book is perfectly in tune with the contemporary trends in classical dance research, in the sense that there is a more sharply focused study of a particular item from a specific point of view, which is a marked development over the conventional trend of a broad survey of dance forms.

I am very much impressed by this work. He took lot of pains in contacting the performers of Kūchipūdi and Mélattūr teams and established dance scholars. His approach in these interviews is worth emulating by the other researchers. One of the most important strengths of his book is the extensive review of past literature on the subject. While giving due credit to all the past researchers, he justified the relevance of his work in the entire body of knowledge available on the subject.

His findings about the subject are original and significant. He could successfully establish that the spirit of the Kūchipūdi dance tradition is artistic, whereas that of the Mélattūr tradition is religious. Though the religiosity of Mélattūr tradition is well known, the way Raju uses this information to contrast with the Kūchipūdi tradition and to identify the mark of identity of Kūchipūdi tradition is new.

The similarities with Bharatanātyam found in Mélattūr tradition are exemplified meticulously by him because of his good background in Kūchipūdi, Bharatanātyam, classical music and tāla system. His particularity to bring home the verbally inexplicable aspects through pictures is evident in the pains he took in getting the pictures drawn by the artist wherever necessary. I commend his effort in bringing out this work in a professional and scholarly manner. This book is a welcome addition to the existing literature and it is a value addition to the scholars and practitioners of South Indian classical dance forms, especially Kūchipūdi and Mélattūr traditions.

Padmasri Dr. Nataraj Ramakrishna

Preface

My interest in the comparison betweem Kūchipūdi and Mélattūr, in general, and Prahlāda Charita Nātakam, in particular, is the culmination of my 28 years of quest about the identity of Kūchipūdi dance tradition into which I got initiated in the year 1980 through my Guru Sri Pasumarti Seeta Ramayya of Visakhapatnam. To begin with, the picture of my quest was hazy. Incidentally, the litrature available in pulbished form on Indian Classical Dance, in general, and Kūchipūdi dance, in particular, also do not provide a methodologically worked out background from where the discussion on the technique of classical dance can be continued, nor does the available literature throw any light for investigation.

I happened to watch the Mélattūr Bhāgavataméla Performance in the year 1994. The impressive performance technique of the Mélattūr Bhagavatars with an approach closely resembling the tradition of Kūchipūdi stimulated several exciting questions in my mind. The Kūchipūdi and Mélattūr performances seemed to be very much similar yet different from each other. It seemed to me that a comparison between these two traditions would also provide with clues to arrive at the characteristic features of Kūchipūdi dance tradition, which was the objective of my quest.

Things progressed quickly after this. To my pleasant surprise, the similarity between the two traditions was already pointed out by most of the scholars. However, they did not touch upon the features of difference between these two traditions. Therefore, I felt that the clues for the identity of the Kūchipūdi and Mélattūr traditions lies in these points of distinction.

For a comparative understanding, I decided to focus on a specific item, Prahlāda Charitra Nātakam, which is common to both

Kūchipūdi and Mélattūr traditions. During 1994-96, I began my filedwork and watched Prahlāda Charitra Nātakam Performance of Mélattūr consecutively for three years, and I revisited the same performance of Kūchipūdi in 1995. My close interaction with the performers of both the teams and my performance study and analysis yielded good results, and some satisfying answers to my enquiry became available.

As is methodologically required by contemporary research in performing arts, visual documentation in the form of still and video photography has been given considerable significance in the present work. Substantiation and illustration through photographs has been provided at appropriate places in this book, though the photo documents included here make only a small part of the entire documentation done by me. Incidentally, photo documents of Mélattūr performance are cited more in this book than for Kūchipūdi because there are many features seemingly unusual for the audience of Mélattūr than for Kūchipūdi, which is familiar to dance audience.

The Mélattūr tradition as performed by Natarajan has been the reference point of comparison with the Kūchipūdi Prahlāda Charitra Natakams. The Comparison and observations made about Kūchipūdi and Mélattūr Bhāgavataméla Nātakams are from the contemporary Mélattūr and Kūchipūdi performances, Many scholars, right from Vissa Appa Rao to Ramandham, have drawn their conclusions based on some cursory observations and they stated that Mélattūr Bhāgavataméla Nātakam was an offshoot of Kūchipūdi Bhagavatam. However, none of them produced any evidence in support of their statements. These scholars started comparing the Yakshagānam technique of both the traditions by talking about the structure and presentation aspects of daruvu system. one of the reasons for these scholars to point out that Mélattūr was an offshoot of Kūchipūdi is because of the existence of pravésa daruvu in both Kūchipūdi and Mélattūr dance forms. And the second reason was the importance of Prahlāda Nātakam in both the forms. Third was female impersonation and using masks. Fourth was fasting by the dancer/actor who plays Narasimha role player in both the forms. Many scholars have not gone into the depth of the subject, like the technique of dance form, style of singing, presentational aspects of the character and makeup and costume of the character.

As per the historical records, artists (Brahmin Bhāgavātars) from Andhra Pradesh had migrated to Mélattūr during 16th century (then the village was known as Achyutāpuram), on the invitation of Atchyutappa Nāyaka. There was no evidence to show that the artists who migrated to Mélattūr were the descendants of Kūchipūdi Brahmin Bhāgavatārs.

After a comparative analysis of both the dance forms, I find a clear distinction between Kūchipūdi and Mélattūr performances, Kūchipūdi is performance oriented, while Mélattūr is spiritual and ritualistic oriented. The present book, thus, is a result of my logical quest into the similarities and differences between Kūchipūdi and Mélattūr traditions, without any digression. Obviously, to focus on a specific item or aspect in the two dance traditions is a new development in dance research when compared to the earlier phase of working on broad issues of an entire dance tradition.

The present work is organized into five chapters. The first chapter, being introductory, attempts to provide the basis of this book. The second and third chapters lay foundation and provide background for this comparison. The first chapter is a comparative study of the repertories of the Mélattūr and the Kūchipūdi dance traditions which provides the hypothesis with which the comparison of Prahlāda Charitra Nātakams in the third and the fourth chapters is taken up. The first chapter is also a comparative introduction to the tradition of Kūchipūdi and Mélattūr dance forms. Review of previous literature on the present subject is also provided in this chapter to emphasize on the relevance of research undertaken.

The second chapter provides cultural, historical and literary backgound against which a comparison in the third and the fourth chapters is carried out. In all these chapters a consistent stream of comparative analysis has been consciously maintained.

The comparison between Prahlāda Charitra Nātakams has been included in the third and the fourth chapters, which are macro and micro level comparisons of Kūchipūdi and Mélattūr Prahlāda Charitra micro Nātakams, respectively.

On account of the state and nature of dance research, heavy reliance on interviews with the tradition bearers of different dance forms and senior scholars in the field becmes inevitable. The third and the fourth chapters deal with performance study of Kūchipūdi and Mélattūr Prahlāda Charitra Nātakams. These chapters are supported by filedwork observations and analysis rather than by references to existing literature, which finds place in the first and second chapters. The fifth chapter is the concluding chapter and it enlists the results of the research undertaken and also offers suggestions for undertaking further research in this area.

Repeating the definitions of art forms, histories, legends of art forms, etc., which we amply dealt with in several books in the past, are avoided in this work.

Acknowledgements

This book is a culmination of a long drawn passion of research into the South Indian dance and theatre forms. I plunged into the research activity due to the inspiration of my childhood friends Mr. Narayana Venu and Ch. Prasada Raju, who persuaded me into the myriad world of classical dance. This book is a revised version of my Ph.D thesis and I owe a great deal to Padmasri Prof. (Dr.) Nataraj Rama Krishna who helped me in a myriad ways; whose role has been more than a teacher. I am privileged to have free access to a person of such eminence who has an in-depth and firsthand experience and understanding of both the dance traditions discussed in the present book. I am thankful to him for writing foreword to this book.

I owe to my teachers Sri. Pasumarti Sitaramayya, Sri. Hemadri Chidambara Dikshitulu, Sri. Vedantam Prahlada Sarma, Sri. Vedantam Radheshyam, Padmasree Dr. Nataraj Ramakrishna, Sri. C. Rama Murty and Smt. Chitra Chandrasekhar, who have immensely enriched me in gaining the knowledge of Kūchipūdi and Bharatanatyam dance traditions.

I am indebted to Late Sri. Chintalapati Varahala Raju for teaching me the nuances of music, specifically the *Tala* system. I owe thanks to Late Sri. Tampella Suryanarayana, who taught me *Karnatic* music and also taught me writing music notations. But for Late Sri. S. Lakshmana Murty, whose drawing skills I exploited in portraying the difficult photographic aspects of performances. My thanks are also due to Dr. P. Nagaraj for his methodological inputs.

My special thanks are due to Prof. A. Raghurama Raju, Department of Philosophy and Prof. R. Siva Prasad, Department of Anthropology, University of Hyderabad, whose constant persuasion and critical comments led me to finish this book in time. I am thankful to Prof. Anuradha who goaded me to complete this task. Thanks are due to Ms. Madhavi for taking pains in proof reading.

I am grateful to Sri Kalaimamani S. Natarajan, Sri. S. Kumar and the other members of Mélattur team; and also to Late Sri. V. Rattayya Sarma, Sri. V. Radheshyam, and the other members of Kūchipūdi team who have shared with me many things that enriched my understanding.

My special thanks to the authorities of Saraswati Mahal Library, Tanjore; Andhra University Library, Visakhapatnam; Pucchalapalli Sundarayya Vijnana Kendram, Hyderabad; Sruti Publications, Chennai; and Indira Gandhi Memorial Library, University of Hyderabad, Hyderabad.

I am deeply indebted to my parents Sri. Munagapati Appala Raju and Late Smt. Sitamma who encouraged me to get into Dance career. I am grateful to my wife, Smt. (Dr.) Vishnu Priya, who have put up with many demands of my research work. I am thankful to my younger brother Sri. Krishnam Raju and his family for their support and warmth. Lastly, I express my sincere thanks to the other members of my family and to many of those others who remain anonymous.

Dr. Munagapati Samba Siva Raju

Contents

List of Plates

LIST OF FIGURES

1

An Introductory Comparison to the Kūchipūdi and Mélattūr Dance Traditions

Though belonging to two different regions, Kūchipūdi and Mélattūr dance forms are often associated with the same classical dance tradition. The Kūchipūdi Bhāgavataméla tradition belongs to the coastal region of Andhra Pradesh, where as the Mélattūr Bhāgavataméla tradition is associated with the famous temple town, Tanjore in Tamil Nadu. The dance associated with the village Kūchipūdi is today an internationally well known Classical dance form and is referred to as Kūchipūdi. Popularity of this form among dance audience and performers has been vibrantly widespread through centuries. Relatively, the Mélattūr Bhāgavataméla tradition, which is also centuries old, is less famous and enjoyed very little spread and popularity beyond Mélattūr till recently[1] . The Mélattūr team started performing their dance dramas outside the village during nineties only. Till then they used to perform only in the village and in the premises of Lord Varadarāja Perumāl temple. They never perform Prahlāda Charitra Nātakam outside the village and it is confined to the temple only.

Vissa Appa Rao is perhaps the first to write a research article on Kūchipūdi published in 1954[2] which introduced this dance tradition from Andhra Pradesh to the outside world. This article distinguishes Kūchipūdi from Bharatanātyam and highlights the former as a dance drama tradition and the latter as a solo dance form. It traces the origin of Kūchipūdi to the Nattuva Mélas of eighth to tenth centuries, present across different regions, like

Kashmir, Andhra Pradesh, Tamil Nadu and Karnataka. The article also claims that these Brahmin Mélas did not take women to play the roles, as they considered their presence may cause deterioration, possibly due to the ritual pollution associated with the menstrual cycle. Interestingly, Appa Rao anticipates the possibility of comparative study of the two forms. He says:

> The dance-dramas of Kūchipūdi and Mélattūr have common characteristics, for instance, the Pravésha daruvu which introduces the characters on the stage; the rakti ragas used in improvised stage in the open street in front a temple; two torch lights; the bag-pipe called the drone; the mridangam and the background music.

Attributing the sources of these common characteristics to the migration of the Kūchipūdi families to Tanjore, he says,

> With the fall of the Vijayanagar Empire these artists migrated to Tanjore and were patronised by the Nayak kings. King Achyutappa Nāyaka, who ruled from 1561 to 1614 AD, granted an agrahāram to hundreds of Brahmin families, in order to encourage and develop the art of dance. The agrahāram was known as Achyutapuram, the modern Mélattūr near Tanjore.

What is not clear here is whether the families that migrated, as mentioned above, were Kūchipūdi artistes at all. Probably, Appa Rao was trying either to raise a doubt or to hint at the branching out of the Kūchipūdi family into Mélattūr by pointing at the common characteristics, quoted above.

Vissa Appa Rao did not clarify whether they originated from the Kūchipūdi families and from which region of Andhra Pradesh they migrated. If they belonged to Kūchipūdi family, what is the source of authenticity for such an inference? He stated that Mélattūr Bhagavatha Méla is an offshoot of Kūchipūdi, because of the nature of similarities such as Pravésa Daruvu (a character introducing oneself), Rakti ragas, torch lights and open space used for their performance. But one cannot come to a conclusion based on a couple of similarities in the performance.

V. Raghavan in his article on Kūchipūdi and Mélattūr claims a more direct relation between them when he asserts that the Mélattūr Bhāgavataméla Nātakam is an offshoot of the Kūchipūdi tradition. He says that the traditional dance drama Bhāgavataméla Nātakam of some of the villages near Tanjore in Tamil Nadu is an offshoot of the Kūchipūdi Bhāgavataméla in Telugu Country.[3]

However, this claim is not substantiated as he does not provide any evidence. If it is an offshoot of Kūchipūdi, there must be some relation with the existing families of Kūchipūdi Bhāgavataméla or Kūchipūdi technique, or there must be some linkage with the present Kūchipūdi art form. Some similarities, however, do not warrant such conclusions.

S.V. Joga Rao published a research article in the Telugu monthly literary journal "Bhārathi" in September 1955 on Mélattūr Bhāgavataméla Nātakams. He also discusses this article in his Ph.D thesis "Andhra Yakshagāna Vangmaya Charitra" (History of the Andhra Yakshagāna literature), while referring to the Mélattūr Bhāgavataméla Nātakams and their performance.[4] He gives a detailed description of both the Kūchipūdi and Mélattūr dance traditions,[5] and also compares the performance details of the Mélattūr form with that of Kūchipūdi. For example, he identifies the following common features:

1. The importance of Prahlāda Nātakam in both the forms.[6]
2. Use of masks.[7]
3. The importance of the dance skills of the female impersonator demonstrated through the pravésa daruvu (the lyric for the entry of the character).[8]
4. Female impersonation.[9]
5. Fasting by the Narasimha Actor.[10]

Like his predecessor Appa Rao, Joga Rao subscribes to the migration of the Kūchipūdi families to Tanjore. In the bibliography section of his Ph.D work Joga Rao cites an article on the subject by V. Raghavan[11] and a thesis submitted for M.Litt of Madras University by Smt. K.Gomati on "The Music of the Nritya Nātakas of South India."[12] But this does not take the discussion any further as there is no supporting evidence.

In 1969 C.R. Acharya, the Bharathācharya (dance teacher) of Kūchipūdi tradition at Darpana in Ahmedabad, wrote a book in Telugu on "Kūchipūdi Ārādhana Nrityamulu" (Kūchipūdi Worship Dances). Mrinalini Sarabhai in her preface claims it to be a 'text book.'[13] This book highlights the ritual worship traditions and the devotional aspect of the Kūchipūdi Dance tradition, thereby emphasizing the devotional origins from the name Bhāgavatulu used in reference to Kūchipūdi performers. But the Kūchipūdi tradition seems to have become more entertainment oriented rather than devotional. Acharya in this book does not present a systematic thesis about the devotional nature of the Kūchipūdi dance tradition, but he refers to interactions between dévadāsis and Kūchipūdi performers in this work. He too refers to the importance of the Prahlāda Nātakam in Kūchipūdi repertoire. Notwithstanding these details Acharya also refers to the Mélattūr performers being descendents of Kūchipūdi performers. In the same discussion on the Prahlāda Nātakam he says,

> "The Brahmin Bhāgavatārs got Achyutapuram (Mélattūr) as an agrahāram by pleasing the Achyutappa Nayaka, the ruler of Tajore for their Prahlāda Nātakam."[14]

In 1977 Sunil Kothari submitted his Ph.D thesis to the Department of Dance in M.S. University of Baroda on "The Dance Drama Tradition of Kūchipūdi Bhāgavataméla Nātaka and Kuravanji, with special reference to Rasa Theory as expounded in Bharata's Nātya Sāstra." He clearly discusses the history of the dance forms, the details of their repertoire, and their technical structure.

He emphasises the Bhakthi movement and its influence on the Kūchipūdi tradition. In this context, he discusses the various legends of Siddhéndra Yōgi and Bhāmākalāpam. Subsequently, he elucidates a detailed description of each number of the repertoire. There is an entire section devoted to Veedhi Bhāgavatam in which different styles of Veedhi Bhāgavatam like the Tūrpu Bāni and other styles are discussed. In the Chapter on technical structure he discusses many important details of the technicalities of the performance, especially the different daruvus (he calls them darus) and observes that the basic technical elements of Kūchipūdi dance drama, Bhāgavataméla Nātakam and Kuravanji are the same. Then he goes on to describe the Nritta, Nritya, the music, rasa and other aspects of the Kūchipūdi performance[15] . He applies these basics to the description of Bhāmākalāpam, its dance-drama form and solo form, Mandūka sabdam, Dasāvatāra sabdam, Ardhanārīswara Sabdam, Tarangams, Kshétrayya padams, etc. Against this background, he discusses Bhāgavataméla Nātakam in a single Chapter[16] . It is in this Chapter that he hints at the branching out of Mélattūr Bhāgavataméla Nātakams from Kūchipūdi. Some observations made by Kothari are relevant for the present comparative study. For example, like Appa Rao and Joga Rao, Kothari also feels that Mélattūr Bhāgavataméla Nātakam is linked with the migration of the Andhra Pradesh dancers to Tamil Nadu[17] . Interestingly Kothari deals, in a great detail, about Narayana Teertha and mentions that,

> "Narayana Teertha was one of those who augmented the Bhāgavata Tradition in the Tanjore district and spread the cult of adoring the Lord with song and dance."[18]

He appropriately mentions that,

> "the same Bhāgavata tradition was responsible also for the cultivation of a dramatic art in which devotional stories composed in the form of songs and set to dance were sung and danced and interpreted in gestures by Brahmin devotees" and he further goes on to observe that, "This tradition which was maintained at the Kūchipūdi village, and which, later on flowered into a dance-drama tradition incorporating the classicism of the tenets of Bharata's Nātya Sāstra spread to Tanjore under the benevolent rule of the Nāyaka Kings."

Then he goes on to describe the different items of the repertoire of Mélattūr Bhāgavataméla Nātakam and at several places refers to the similarities between Kūchipūdi and Mélattūr Bhāgavataméla Nātakams. He goes to the extent of saying that,

> "As a matter of fact these dance-dramas are an offshoot of the Kūchipūdi dance-dramas with a difference in the technique of dance, the style being that of what has come to be known as contemporary Bharatanātyam technique."[19]

Interestingly he even lists several dissimilarities between the two forms.

> "It is different in character than the rounded, embellished with quick silver movements and spring like quality of pure dance of Kūchipūdi nritta. It is more austere, has geometrical form, exquisite lineaments, arabesques, triangles, parabolas, horizontal lines, vertical ones and has three kalas performed in three tempos, vilambitha, madhyama, drutha."[20]

He further compared both the dance forms and made certain points that the Mélattūr Bhagavatha Méla must have migrated from Kūchipūdi initially, and, later, after some years, the technique must have changed with the regional influence of Bharatanātyam dance form. He tried to compare both the forms and found some similarities in the technique. But he did not show any evidence to strengthen his statement that the Mélattūr Bhagavatha Méla is an offshoot of Kūchipūdi.

Chintha Ramanadham's "The Kūchipūdi School of Yakshagāna-Literary: traditional and technical perspective" too discusses the Kūchipūdi and Mélattūr dance forms. Interestingly there is a section of the thesis with the title "Kūchipūdi Mélattūr Bhāgavataméla Nātakamulu: Oka Samgraha Paramarsa" (Kūchipūdi and Mélattūr Bhāgavataméla Nātakams–a brief overview).[21] In this 'brief overview' he joins all the authors reviewed above in stating that the Mélattūr Bhāgavata Méla families are the descendants of the Kūchipūdi families. Ramanadham is positive in concluding in favour of the migration of Kūchipūdi to Mélattūr. He quotes two lines from the Prahlāda Pattabhisékha sabdam of the Kūchipūdi tradition in which the name of Achyutāpuram is mentioned. As Achyutāpuram is the other name of Mélattūr, Ramanadham gives this as an evidence for a possible migration of the Kūchipūdi families to Mélattūr. He also mentions that the Bhāgavatārs to whom Mélattūr was donated[22] as an agraharam[23] are said to be Kūchipūdi Bhāgavatārs themselves. Further, he points out that some of the family names of the Mélattūr Bhāgavatārs coincide with those of the Kūchipūdi families. He also quotes a conversation between Chinta Krishna Murthy of Kūchipūdi troupe, who visited Mélattūr in 1969 as part of interstate cultural exchange programme and a few elders of the Mélattūr families told Chinta Krishna Murthy that the ancestors of the Mélattūr family were from Kūchipūdi who came hundreds of years ago for royal patronage and settled down in Mélattūr. On the basis of this information Ramanadham concludes that Kūchipūdi dance tradition migrated to Mélattūr. Here it may be noted that Ramanadham belongs to the Kūchipūdi family of dancers and Chinta Krishna Murthy is Ramanadham's father. However, Ramanadham's observations with regard to the migration only strengthen the theory of a strongly possible genetic relation between Kūchipūdi and Mélattūr traditions.

After that Ramanadham proceeds to list several similarities between the Kūchipūdi and Mélattūr dance traditions as a further evidence for his theory of migration. Amongst these there is a controversial arguement that both the Kūchipūdi and Mélattūr Mélams performed Bhāmākalāpam in the beginning. But there is absolutely no evidence to support that the Mélattūr Mélams performed Bhāmākalāpam. Within the Kūchipūdi tradition too there is no evidence conclusively to say that Bhāmākalāpam is historically the first item of the Kūchipūdi repertoire, as assumed by Ramanadham.[24]

He brings comparison between the annual performances by the Kūchipūdi Mélams in the pandals raised in front of the Ramalingéswara Temple, one of the two main temples of the village of Kūchipūdi, and the annual performances by the Mélattūr Mélam near the Narasimha temple of the Mélattūr village.[25] Whether the sacral strictness found in the Mélattūr performances of Narasimha Jayanthi is found in the same intensity and with a similar attitude in the Kūchipūdi performance during the Sri Ramalingéswara Kalyanam is to be carefully verified. Mélattūr performances are clearly done for the temple deity. The Kūchipūdi performances in front of the temple are not necessarily for the temple deity.

Another similarity, pointed out by Ramanadham, is the presence of the comic supporting artistes called Hangudārs or Vanthadārs in both the traditions. He points out that the character of Kontekōnangi (the mischievous guy) was also the common feature for both the traditions; the Kūchipūdi people excluded this character from their tradition to avoid 'unsophisticatedness' (except Bhāmākalāpam, where there is such a character).[26]

Further, as mentioned by Ramanadham, is the presence of a Sabdam or Jatiswaram or Ashtapadi or Tarangam or Tillana (all solo items) after the Pravésha Daruvu (the entry lyric) of the female character in both Kūchipūdi and Mélattūr traditions. According to Ramanadham, this item is included to demonstrate the dancing talent of the female impersonator. However, items like Jatiswaram, Ashtapadi, Tarangam and Tillana mentioned by Ramanadham are not found in Mélattūr performances.

Another point mentioned by Ramanadham in his comparison is that both Kūchipūdi and Mélattūr follow the Nātya Sāstra and Abhinaya Darpana but adds that the Kūchipūdi tradition also follows Jāyappa Sénani's Nritta Ratnāvali but does not attempt to support his statement. Does this information point to the history or period of branching out of these two possible genetic cousins? This needs to be carefully investigated further.

Ramanadham mentions fasting by both the Kūchipūdi and Mélattūr performers of Narasimha, Rukmāngada, etc., as another point of similarity. He concludes his comparison by pointing out major differences between the traditions, namely, the Kūchipūdi Mélam has been a touring Mélam from the beginning and Mélattūr Mélam has always been confined to Mélattūr.

It may be observed that Ramanadham, who has been very keen in enlisting various similarities and the major difference like the touring and non-touring aspects of the two traditions, somehow misses to see that the more important difference between the two traditions is their repertoires. The large and variegated repertoire of Kūchipūdi is conspicuously different from the small monolithic repertoire of the Mélattūr tradition. The Yakshagānams, which are the only item of the repertoire of the Mélattūr Bhāgavataméla Nātakams, is shared by the Kūchipūdi tradition. But Kūchipūdi repertoire contains lot more items like Bhāmākalāpam, Tarangams, Adhyātma Rāmāyana Kīrtanas, Sabdams, Astapadis, etc. This aspect of repertoire which makes the two traditions look glaringly different has been somehow overlooked by all the authors reviewed above. Quite often the Kūchipūdi tradition is identified with certain items like Bhāmākalāpam and Tarangams which are totally absent in the Mélattūr tradition. Moreover, the fact that the repertoire of one form is enormously larger than the other cannot be ignored as insignificant. The identity of the Kūchipūdi form comes from a combined identity evolving out of its entire broad repertoire, and the identity of the Mélattūr form from the specific limited items of devotional Yakshagānams. Under such circumstances this point of difference should be taken as an important point of analysis in any comparative study between the two forms. One may say that the Kūchipūdi tradition has been artistically oriented whereas the Mélattūr tradition has been ritualistic and devotional. Ramanadham, like the others reviewed above, does not attempt to identify any reason for the differences between the two comparable, possibly genetically related, art forms.

In his discussion on the comparison between the Kūchipūdi and Mélattūr traditions Ramanadham proceeds to review the text of the Ushā Parinayam and Prahlāda Charitram composed by Mélattūr Venkata Rāma Sāstry providing a brief and quick comparative analysis of the performances and texts of both these plays in the Kūchipūdi and Mélattūr traditions. The Prahlāda Charitram was subjected to a comparative study by Ramanadham, though for just two pages, in his thesis on the Kūchipūdi Yakshagānam.[27] All the authors reviewed above considered

Prahlāda Charitram to be an important item of both Kūchipūdi and Mélattūr traditions. Ramanadham's choice of this as one of the two topics of comparative study reaffirms this widely accepted significance of Prahlāda Charitram.

Ramanadham was basically a traditional artist of Kūchipūdi Bhāgavata Méla. He pointed out the similarities in the two dance forms and further attempted to say that Mélattūr form is an offshoot of Kūchipūdi dance based on his observations. If Mélattūr form is an offshoot of the Kūchipūdi form, then why the technique is not of Kūchipūdi and why there is no variegated repertoire as in Kūchipūdi, and, most importantly, why the Bhāmākalāpam performance, which was supposed to have been written by Siddhéndra Yogi, is not seen in Mélattūr tradition? We can understand the regional influence on the technique to some extent, but not completely. Therefore, it is difficult to concur with Ramanadham.

A further link between the two forms is elicited by V. Raghavan.[28] He says that,

> "Traditionally the Kūchipūdi performance teams were called "Bhāgavata Mélams of Kūchipūdi"; individually Kūchipūdi performers were called "Bhāgavatulu".

The performance was also referred to as a Bhāgavatam. These words are used in reference to the Mélattūr tradition also. The performing teams of Mélattūr are referred to as Mélattūr Bhāgavata Mélams. Individually, Mélattūr performers are called Bhāgavatārs and their performances are also called as Bhāgavatam.

All the Mélattūr performers are Brahmin males and the tradition is not open to non-Brahmins or even to Brahmin females. Though the Kūchipūdi tradition is today open to all castes and genders the historical fact is that it was also for a long time limited to the Brahmin males and was not open to others.

More interestingly, both Kūchipūdi and Mélattūr traditions, being theatrical dance traditions, stand apart from many Indian classical dances. The genre of both Kūchipūdi and Mélattūr performances are broadly categorised under Yakshagāna/Vīdhi Bhāgavatam/ Vīdhinātakam.[29]

Kapilā Vātsāyan in her 'Traditional Indian Theatre Multiple Streams'[30] says that,

> "In Andhra Pradesh and Tamil Nadu are prevalent many dance-drama forms which are called by varying names- Bhāgavataméla, Kūchipūdi, Bhāmākalāpam, Yakshagāna, etc. Others such as Veethinaatakam of Andhra Pradesh and Terukoothu of Tamil Nadu are today called the street theatre forms... While it is possible to treat each of these separately, as each has a distinctive character, there are many overlapping areas of theme and content which make them members of a large family. ... All these belong to the generic literary form called the Yakshagāna which emerged in Andhra Pradesh, Tamil Nadu and Karnataka."

Though we find several solo and non-drama items in the Kūchipūdi repertoire, most of the items of the contemporary Kūchipūdi performances are non-dramatic in nature. We still find several reminiscences of the theatrical nature of the Kūchipūdi tradition even in the contemporary Kūchipūdi performances. For example, in a small episode of Bhāmākalāpam (item) performed on the stage today, a small significant prose conversation, dramatic in nature, is included. This feature, which is not found in any other solo dance form of India, obviously indicates the theatrical background of the Kūchipūdi tradition. The item called Vināyaka Koutwam which is performed in the contemporary Kūchipūdi stage concerts is in fact a mask dance which was a part of the traditional Kūchipūdi dance drama performance as one of the early invocation items.[31] There are several such features in the contemporary performances that are obvious reminders of its theatrical background. More importantly, there are still a large number of traditional performers of Kūchipūdi who clearly subscribe to the idea of Kūchipūdi tradition being basically theatrical and there are still many of them who continue to perform the traditional Bhāgavatams[32] (theatrical Yakshagānam type dances). As narrated by the traditional performers, and as is witnessed even today in the traditional performances, the traditional Kūchipūdi Bhāgavatam performances were performed on a level ground in the midst of an encircling audience (usually in a semicircle in front of the performers). Help was taken of a make shift screen behind which characters entered and exited. While the screen itself was held on either side by members of the Bhāgavata Mélam , there was the Sūtradhāra[33] (Plate-I) standing in front of the screen playing on cymbals and singing the Pravésha Daruvu (entry lyric) and introducing characters, making intervening comments, etc. If there is a Nattuvanār[34] (Plate-I) today in the place of Sūtradhāra, it is obviously due to the influence of solo repertoire of the entertaining dancers (traditionally the team directors/managers stand close to the dancer). All these features of the traditional Kūchipūdi performance indicate its basic theatrical nature.

Plate-I: Védantam Prahlāda Sarma and P.V.G. Krishna Sarma as Nattuva Hangu and Sūtradhārudu (Source: Sangeetha Natak Akademy Archives, New Delhi).

What is interesting is that all these features, like the makeshift screen, the Sūtradhāra, prose conversation, etc., are found even in the Mélattūr performances. For that matter, the Mélattūr performance even today is of Bhāgavatam type only. The solo items found in the Kūchipūdi tradition are not at all found in the Mélattūr form. The question here is whether the Mélattūr Brahmins had confined themselves to temple only after migrating to Mélattūr? Or whether Kūchipūdi incorporated solo numbers into its repertoire after the migration of the Mélattūr team? Or else both the forms might have been artistically oriented before the migration and Mélattūr Bhāgavatārs might have shifted to the devotional approach due to the patronage of the Varadarāja Perumāl temple and King Achyutappa Nāyaka.

The Kūchipūdi dance conforms to the tenets of Bhārata's Nātya Sāstra and the other classical texts on dance. It is argued that Kūchipūdi alone has the comprehensive inclusion of dance, drama and music, which are discussed as constituting Nātya in Bhārata's treatise. Even the components like Pūrvaranga, described at length by Bharata, are found in Kūchipūdi. Parallel to the Purvarangam[35] in the performance of the Kūchipūdi tradition the Mélattūr tradition has a similar performance called Todaimangalam[36]. The dance style of Kūchipūdi is strictly according to the instruction of Bharata in terms of various other elements like Hastas (Hand Gestures), Karanas (Body postures), Grivas (Neck movements and facial directions), etc. It is noteworthy that the Kūchipūdi performers were given intense courses in Sanskrit literature and Sāstrās, including Nātya Sāstra, as part of their early childhood initiation into the tradition[37]. All these arguments that favour classical identity of the Kūchipūdi equally hold good for the Mélattūr tradition also. At the same time, the features of Kūchipūdi (which are argued as indicative of the folk element), like flexibility, spontaneous response to the audience, lack of rigid script, extempore improvisations, involvement of the audience, reflection of regional culture and family custom, etc., also are shared equally by the Mélattūr tradition.

The fact that the musical style used in Kūchipūdi and Mélattūr is Carnatic is not surprising, as both are south Indian forms and the classical musical style prevalent in both Andhra Pradesh and Tamil Nadu is Carnatic. It is pertinent to note that in both Kūchipūdi and Mélattūr forms the text is in Telugu. It is here that some of the aspects of historical 'kinship' of the two forms come out. Though the Mélattūr performers today are Tamil speakers with a weak competence in Telugu, the oral histories recounted by some of the performers reiterate that they are the descendants of the Telugu speaking families of Kūchipūdi[38] leads to some interesting historical speculations. It is on the basis of this information that several scholars hurried to conclude that the Mélattūr Bhāgavataméla branched out from "Kūchipūdi main stock".

But some of the Mélattūr performers themselves disagree with these theories and claim that they migrated from the present Nellore District of Andhra Pradesh[39] and these Nellore families of dancers had nothing to do with the Kūchipūdi Bhāgavatha Méla[40]. However, all the similarities between the two forms, as enlisted already, may not support the second claim of the Mélattūr performers. Though the "Kūchipūdi main stock" theory may not be valid, some kind of kinship between the Kūcḥipūdi and Mélattūr forms cannot be ruled out completely. The kinship has to be not only typological but should also be genetic. Though the theory that Kūchipūdi is the mother of all Bhāgavatams may be set aside, as only a good example of the old monogenesis theories, the possibility of Kūchipūdi and Mélattūr forms being the branches of same origin cannot be ruled out.

The genetic kinship of the two apart, even the typological kinship gives rise to a natural question of the reasons for the differences in terms of popularity and spread between the two closely related forms. Another issue that emerges is the impact of the Tamil environment on a form with Telugu text and with an acknowledged Telugu origin.

MARKS OF DISTINCTION

The first point of distinction is the repertoire of the two art forms. The repertoire of the Kūchipūdi art form is enormously larger than that of Mélattūr. The Kūchipūdi dance form today is characterised by a combination of the features of its variegated repertoire. Looked from this point of view the Mélattūr art form appears to be clearly different from the Kūchipūdi art form.

The Kūchipūdi dance form is almost identified with one of the most popular items of its repertoire called Bhāmākalāpam. For many, Kūchipūdi dance form comes to mind only in the form of Bhāmākalapam. This is a long dance-drama performed traditionally for seven long nights. The Brahmin male dancers of Kūchipūdi impersonate Satyabhāma, second in the rank of lord Sri Krishna's eight principal consorts (first being Rukmini), the most vocal, possessive, assertive and pampered of all his consorts. The text of Bhāmākalāpam contains a conversation between Satyabhāma and one of her attendants, Mādhavi, which reveals several inner delicate complex feelings of Satyabhāmā's possessive love for Sri Krishna that are brought out emphatically in Kūchipūdi performance. This runs in a series of lyrics called Daruvus and is divided into seven different episodes called 'Pattus.'[41]

The first episode is Jadapattu. This item is a household name in Andhra Pradesh and audience, both men and women, enjoy equally watching this item. For the artist this item is an opportunity to exhibit his skill in impersonating the female character.[42]

This significant item of Kūchipūdi repertoire is conspicuously missing in the Mélattūr repertoire. One way of explaining this absence, if the genetic kinship of the two art forms is accepted, is to say that the item of Bhāmākalāpam entered the Kūchipūdi repertoire after these two genetic kins branched out from each other. This item clearly works as a mark of distinction between the Mélattūr and Kūchipūdi traditions. It is not that there is no impersonation of female character in the Mélattūr tradition; since Mélattūr performers are all males, there is bound to be impersonation of female characters even in this dance form. In fact, Mélattūr dancers impersonate several female characters such as Līlāvathi, Bhūmidévi (all in Prahlāda Charitram), Chandramati (in Harischandra), Ushā (in Ushā Parinayam), etc.

But the female character impersonation in Bhāmākalāpam, that is, the impersonation of Satyabhāma, is a class by itself and this is what gives the mark of distinction to Kūchipūdi.[43] Bhāma in

Bhāmākalapam, unlike the female characters in the Mélattūr items, is not only a major character but also the heroine of Bhāmākalapam's story. In fact, the entire Bhāmākalapam is a one character show with Bhāma present on the stage from the beginning to the end. Mādhavi, the only other character appearing on the stage along with Bhamā plays only the minor role of an attendant - companion-confidant.[44]

Sri Krishna, another major character, appears only for a few minutes towards the end. In Mélattūr repertoire there is no such item which can be called as a single woman character show. It should also be noted that Bhāmā, unlike Rādha (of the Krishna items of the North-Indian classical dance), who is one of the Gopa Sakhis (Cowherd - girlfriends) of Krishna, is impressively unique even from a national perspective. Bhāma is a Swīya Nāyika (his married wife). All the nuances of married life get reflected in Bhāmā's romance, which is in clear contrast with non-marital romance of Rādha-Krishna items of the North-Indian dances. The absence of such a significant and unique item of Kūchipūdi tradition in the Mélattūr form is obviously an important line of distinction between the two traditions.

Another item with which the Kūchipūdi dance form is usually identified is Tarangams. Now-a-day, it is a regular practice to perform Tarangams in the form of dance on brass plate, with lamps in the hands and vessel on the head, etc. Acrobatic fetes are being recognised by the outsiders as the characteristic features of the Kūchipūdi dance. Though this acrobatic skill demonstration is an essential feature of neither Tarangams nor Kūchipūdi tradition, Tarangams themselves are doubtlessly the characteristic and unique feature of the Kūchipūdi tradition. Tarangams belong to the Bhajan tradition. This item mainly consists of the repetitive singing of the descriptive names of Lord Krishna as a part of '*Nāmarūpaguna līlāsankīrtana*' of the Bhakti tradition. During the singing of each one of such descriptive names, several episodes from the story of Krishna are enacted (mimed) by the dancer.

The musical composition used in Tarangams is typically in bhajan style with a blend of the classical and Ātakachéri (dance music) styles of music. Such an important item of the Kūchipūdi tradition is glaringly missing in the Mélattūr repertoire of dance performances. Interestingly, in Mélattūr, Tarangams are found in the tradition of singing a Bhajan.[45] Since the words Bhāgavatam, Bhāgavatārs, etc., used in reference to Kūchipūdi and Mélattūr traditions refer to the Bhakti movement, it is quite natural to find bhakti-centered items in both Kūchipūdi and Mélattūr. But the availability of dance tradition of Tarangams in Kūchipūdi and their non-availability in Mélattūr tradition is a clear marker of distinction between the two dance forms. In case of the validity of the theory of genetic kinship of the two forms, this difference in the case of Tarangams may be explained, just as in the case of Bhāmākalapam, by the entry of Tarangams into the repertọire of the Kūchipūdi tradition after the migration of the Mélattūr group form Andhra Pradesh to Tamil Nadu. As the date of Tarangams is clearly known today as of 17th century (the author of Tarangams Narayanatirtha belongs to 17th century), we can easily conclude that the proposed branching out of the Mélattūr form from the Kūchipūdi must have taken place prior to 17th century.[46] However, the availability of singing tradition of Tarangams in the Mélattūr village could be due to the migration of Tarangams to Mélattūr later to the migration of the Mélattūr Bhāgavata Méla.

Another significant item of the Kūchipūdi repertọire is Sabdam. Sabdam consists of long vocal recitals of the syllables of the mridangam (the rhythmic accompaniment used in the South Indian [Carnatic] music and also in Kūchipūdi dance form) mixed with a few lyrical lines consisting usually of rhetorical praises of kings or deities. For example, the text of the Bhōsala Sabdam is as follows:

"Dhākita kitajham

tadhi takitajham

taka dhiku

tāri tāri jhām tari ki da ta ka

tā dhi ki da taka taka dhina tōm, tehi da tta thōm.

Rājasri bhōsala kula chandra

rati pati sundara rāja Narēndra

rāja tulaja maharāja tanuja

pratāpa simha sūtramā salām

dhissalām dhi dhi ssalām.

From line number 1 to 5 may be seen as the syllables of Mridangam. Line no. 6 to 10 may be translated as follows:

Oh! King, who is the moon of (the ocean of) the lineage of Bhonsle,

Handsome like Cupid, king of kings, Son of the Emperor, Raja Tulja.

Oh! Pratāpasimha the great, salutations to you, salutations again, salutations again and again.

Even this item had been missing in the Mélattūr tradition till recently. Interestingly, though it is said that Mélattūr Venkatarama Sastry[47] of the 18th century composed several Sabdams, the "Prahlāda Pattābhishékha Sabdam" is the only one being performed by the Mélattūr team. An interesting aspect of this Sabdam is that, unlike the above mentioned Sabdams which are just rhetorical praises and non-narrative, this is a long narrative composition containing a narration of the Prahlāda Charitra Story.[48] Rāmāyana Sabdam, Prahlāda Pattābhishékha Sabdam, Dasāvatāra Sabdam, Mandūka Sabdam and Mandódari Sabdams are the narrative Sabdams of the Kūchipūdi tradition.

The musical composition of Sabdams is rhythm dominated, usually in fast rhythm. The central tone and tenor of the composition is that of the pompous medieval court recital of praise addressing the king and adapted as such into the Yakshagāna tradition. Usually, there is no scope for variations in either melody or rhythm in a single Sabdam. The performance of Sabdams as a dance item in Mélattūr tradition is absent. However, there is a tradition of singing Sabdams which is interesting.[49] Whether, there existed a tradition of performing Sabdams during the time of Mélattūr Venkatarāma Sāstry is not clear. However, since Sabdam is the only item, apart from Bhāgavatam performances, that is common between the Kūchipūdi and Mélattūr traditions, this may be expected to provide some more clues about the kinship between Kūchipūdi and Mélattūr traditions.

Did the two traditions branch out from each other after sharing the item of the Sabdam for some time? There is a version that the Kūchipūdi performers visited Mélattūr somewhere during the 19th century and brought Sabdams to Andhra region along with them. Especially, the availability of the Prahlāda Pattābhishékha Sabdam composed by Mélattūr Venkatarama Sastry in the repertoire of Kūchipūdi tradition gives scope for such conjecturing. Alternatively, this version may be accepted only in the case of the specific Sabdam, viz., Prahlāda Pattābhishékha Sabdam, and all the other Sabdam compositions of the Kūchipūdi tradition may be inferred to have been original to the Kūchipūdi group. Especially, the Krishnarāya Sabdam of the Kūchipūdi tradition indicates the existence of Sabdam compositions in Kūchipūdi tradition even during the sixteenth century. Then the commonness of the Sabdams of the Kūchipūdi and Mélattūr traditions can be explained only on the basis of the common Yakshagāna tradition shared by both of them. This may have to do with their genetic kinship too. But a remarkable dissimilarity between the Kūchipūdi and Mélattūr Sabdams is the non-availability of the praises to the kings in the Mélattūr tradition and availability of the same in the Kūchipūdi tradition. This could be explained on the basis of the fact that Mélattūr tradition has always been a temple oriented tradition never reaching the court halls of the kings. Kūchipūdi group on the other hand has a clear cut record of having performed in the courts of several kings right from the 15th century. The oldest available record of the Kūchipūdi tradition, the "Machupalli Kaifiat", mentions the performance by the Kūchipūdi group in the court of Viranarasimha Rayalu[50]. On the whole, it can be said that Sabdams give the characteristic mark of identity to the Kūchipūdi tradition along with all the remaining items of its huge repertoire of solo items and the Mélattūr tradition, which is glaringly devoid of a solo repertoire, stands distinct from its closely resembling possible cousin. The difference in terms of approach of the two traditions towards the courts of the kings is worth noting.

Another interesting distinct item of the Kūchipūdi repertoire is Adhyātma Rāmāyana Kīrtanas. This is a solo narrative dance performance. The script used is the devotional lyrics that are highly popular in the traditional households of Andhra containing the story of Rāmāyana as in Adhyātma Rāmāyana, which is a devotional popular version of Vālmīki's Rāmāyana[51]. This script is almost similar to the script of Krishna Lila Tarangini, which is the lyrical composition of Bhāgavatam's Dwadasaskhandha (twelfth canto, the story of Krishna). Each of the lyrics depicts a particular episode of Rāmāyana. This lyric is composed in classical Carnatic in an Ata Kachéri (dance concert) style adding suitable Jatis. A single dancer enacts different characters of the episode. The narrative performance tradition is historically supposed to be the earlier form of the Yakshagāna drama style. Again the Adhyātma Rāmāyana Kīrtana is conspicuously absent in the Mélattūr form. This absence is interesting because Mélattūr form containing devotional items in its repertoire can naturally be expected to contain such a devotional item. Again this absence can be explained by conjecturing that this item might have entered Kūchipūdi repertoire later to the branching out of the Mélattūr tradition from the Kūchipūdi and the spread of Adhyātma Rāmāyana Kīrtana as a dance item must have been limited to the Andhra region. There is another explanation, Prof. Nataraja Ramakrishna opines that Adhyātma Rāmāyana Kīrtanas were originally part of the Dévadāsi temple dance repertoire and the Kūchipūdi dancers must have borrowed it from the Dévadāsi tradition.[52]

This opinion is supported by the evidence provided by Sri C.R. Acharya that the Kūchipūdi artistes interacted with the Dévadāsis or the temple dancers during a certain stage in terms of give and take of dance-techniques. Acharya feels that the temple dancers learnt several aspects of the Kūchipūdi technique from the Kūchipūdi artistes[53]. This interaction can be expected to have resulted in the Kūchipūdi artistẹs learning the Adhyātma Rāmāyana Kīrtana from the Dévadāsi temple dancers.

Another important item of the Kūchipūdi repertoire is the Ashtapadi. In fact, Ashtapadis composed by Jayadéva formed a part of the repertoires of almost all dance forms of India from Manipuri, Kathak and Odissi to Kūchipūdi, Bharatanātyam and Mōhinīattam. Like in all other Indian classical dance forms even in Kūchipūdi Jayadéva Ashtapadi is a solo item. Usually, this is considered to be an item giving scope for the dancer to bring out his or her Sātwikābhinaya skills because these lyrics contain several psychological moods of Rādha and other Gopis. In each Ashtapadi performance, sancharis are also enacted based on certain lines of the lyrics. Since these lyrics are considered to be containing Madhura Bhakti (devotion in the form of man and woman love), the dance performance has some amount of devotional significance also. It is interesting to see that in spite of this devotional image, this item which is shared by many Indian Dance forms is not found in the Mélattūr form. Here, the explanation of later entry of the item into Kūchipūdi repertoire cannot be sufficient. When the Ashtapadis were borrowed into so many different dance traditions of the country, it is logical to be curious as to why it did not enter the Mélattūr form. The only possible answer is the absence of the development of a solo repertoire in the Mélattūr tradition and the theatrical form being the only component of this tradition.

The next important item of the Kūchipūdi repertoire is the Kshétrayya Padams. Kshétrayya Padams are, to some extent, similar to Jayadévā's Ashtapadis. This is also a solo item. Like Ashtapadis these too contains the Parakīya Vipralambha Sringāra of Krishna's love. But Kshétrayya's Padams are different from Ashtapadis in several other ways. The Nāyikas are neither Radha nor Gopis. These Nāyikas are significantly unnamed and their community background is left undescribed and insignificant. Compared to Jayadéva's Ashtapadis, these lyrics are more intensively erotic and less devotional.[54] In fact, these lyrics are believed to have been composed by Kshétrayya as scripts for the

Royal Court dancers–women in the Court of Vijaya Raghava Nayaka the 17th century king of Tanjore.[55] Kshétrayya is a poet-singer, who, both as a musician and lyricist, made path breaking contributions to both Carnatic music and Telugu poetry. Kshétrayya is believed to have contributed greatly towards the emergence of Carnatic music in its present form. These lyrics are known for the availability of a variety of Nāyikas, including the Ashtavidha Nāyikas.[56]

His lyrics are admired by dancers and literary critics alike, for the ability of the author in bringing out several secret delicate aspects of womanly eros with several meticulous details and with a great variety, compared to Ashtapadis and Tarangams–which are in Sanskrit. The major point of attraction in Kshétrayya's Padams is the day-today-ness of their content, colloquialism and popular idiom in their language, freshness and delicacy in their diction and native colour in the culture described in them[57] . This gives enormous scope for sātvikābhinaya[58] and this is what attracts a dancer towards Kshétrayya's Padamas. How the item entered Kūchipūdi repertoire from the Royal court of Tanjore is not clear. Muvva, the native place of Kshétrayya, the author of the Padams, is close to Kūchipūdi village. Did the Kshétrayya Padams reach Kūchipūdi from Muvva? Did the Kūchipūdi performers borrow this item from the Royal court of Tanjore? Or, did they borrow this from Dévadāsi temple dancers (in whose repertoire this was an important item along with Jāvalis[59])?

But the fact that the Kūchipūdi performers performed Kshétrayya Padams for a long time (probably right from 17th century) is mentioned in the memoirs of the traditional Kūchipūdi artistes.[60] It is described by the traditional Kūchipūdi performers and by those who witnessed the traditional performances of Kshétrayya Padams that these lyrics were originally performed by the Dévadāsis in the sitting posture without much movement of the legs or the feet. Facial expressions, especially Sātwikābhinaya in the face, were what matteres the most. To bring out all the minute feelings depicted in the lyrics into the facial expressions was the criterion on the basis of which the performer's talent was measured. The fact that most of the Kshétrayya Padams were composed by Kshétrayya in Triputa Talam[61] and in vilambita (slow pace) rhythm indicates the intention of the author to use these lyrics only for a Sātwikābhinaya (usually in sitting posture) dominated performance. No other poet-singer employed Triputa Talam in such a rich and central way as Kshétrayya did. He exploited the scope for Sātwikābhinaya in Triputa Talam compositions to the fullest extent. Probably the performance of Kshétrayya Padam accompanied by leg movements emerged along with the stage performance of these lyrics (i.e., during the modern times).[62] Or, probably, both the sitting and the leg moving forms of the performance of Kshétrayya Padam existed simultaneously from the beginning.

However, the fact that the dominance of Sātwikābhinaya of minute feminine delicate and erotic feelings was the central feature of the Kshétrayya Padams cannot be denied. Absence of this item in Mélattūr is again a curious fact, since Mélattūr is geographically only 18 kms away from Tanjore and the Mélattūr form, from all the known records, was in its boom during the time when Kshétrayya was composing these lyrics and its music. One explanation which may help us in understanding this interesting immunity of Mélattūr tradition to the influence of Kshétrayya Padams could be that Mélattūr never had a court performance record and Kshétrayya Padams have always been associated with court performances. Another reason could be the disinterest of the Mélattūr tradition in such an overwhelmingly erotic item that does not fit into the devotional frame of the entire repertoire of that tradition.

This explanation applies to another item of distinction between Kūchipūdi and Mélattūr, namely, Jāvalis. Jāvalis are erotic lyrics known for their occurrence in the repertoire of sexually entertaining dancers. Kūchipūdi performers performed even these lyrics. How and why these entered Kūchipūdi repertoire is not clear. One possible source is the interaction between the Kūchipūdi performers with Dévadāsis, who, in course of time, acquired certain features of the erotic entertainment in their dances. For the same reasons as discussed above, it is natural for the Mélattūr tradition whose repertoire is in a strictly devotional frame to be insulated to the entry of items like Jāvalis.

The characteristic feature of the Kūchipūdi tradition lies in accommodating, absorbing and adopting theatrical (e.g. Bhāgavatam), solo (e.g. Ashtapadis), devotional (e.g.Tarangams), erotic (e.g. Kshétrayya Padams), classical (e.g. Bhāmākalapam), folk (e.g. Ardhanārīswaram, Dādinamma), court oriented (e.g. Sabdams), temple oriented (e.g. Adhyātmarāmāyana Kīrtana), street oriented (e.g. Vīdhibhāgavatam), and stage oriented features (e.g. Modern Kūchipūdi items components) into its repertoire. This character of Kūchipūdi dance form is explained by Nataraj Ramakrishna as related to the poor financial state of the performers.[63] In an interview he also traces this to their travelling from one place to another.[64] Apart from these opinions, there is a need to make an in-depth study elucidating various contributing factors that shaped this nature of flexibility. In this context, there is a need to take the discussion away from the religious realm, though not necessarily delinking from it, and bring into the centre stage the artistic aspects.

One may conclude that what characterizes the Mélattūr tradition is not its repertoire, not its performance but the spirit which worked behind the immunity of the tradition to the adaptations of items such as those adapted by its possible genetic cousin Kūchipūdi. As against the artistic priority of the Kūchipūdi tradition, Mélattūr tradition's priority seems to be intensely religious, tradition oriented and devotional. This, however, does not mean that the Mélattūr tradition has no artistic priority. When it comes to choosing between loose flexibility and traditional strictness, the Mélattūr performer chooses the later. In other words, the priority of the Mélattūr team is ritualistic rather than artistic.

The first available record about Kūchipūdi dance tradition (which was quoted earlier while talking about Sabdams), the Machupalli kaifiat, a local record of Machupalli[65] (1502 A.D.), describes the performance of an episode of the atrocities committed by one Sammeta Guravaraju, a local chief (Sardar), of

Siddhavatam in front of Viranarashimha Rayalu. How such a social theme could enter the repertoire of Kūcipūdi tradition during such early times is not clear. However, there is a scope to include such episodes into any Yakshagāna performance as there is no fixed text. This lack of rigidity facilitates the possibility of spontaneous improvisation. Common issues concerning local people, their habits and culture do get their place, particularly in intervals that provide humour, to dilute the impact of the emotionally pitched seriousness of the performance. This perhaps may be the reason for the inclusion of Sammeta Guravaraju episode described in the Machupalli Kaifiat. This establishes that the inclination of the Kūchipūdi tradition from the beginning has been towards a flexible folk oriented entertainment rather than strictly religious and devotional format. In contrast, the Mélattūr performance does not have any such digressions from the conventional text being performed.

The adaptation of Pagativeshalu[66] (day time guises), which lead to the adaptation of items such as Ardhanārīswarudu and Dādinamma into the Kūchipūdi repertoire would not be possible if the Kūchipūdi tradition were religious and not entertainment oriented. Pagativéshālu (day time guises) is basically a humour centred entertainment performance which contains episodes from the night time performances such as Yakshagānam. Kūchipūdi performers did not hesitate to adopt such a performance, when they found it to be entertaining.

From the point of view that dance is basically an art form, and that the artistic priority is primary for an art form, the theory of artistic priority of Kūchipūdi tradition may look to be a statement of the obvious. But if we take the fact that the Kūchipūdi performers share the name of Bhāgavatulu with the Mélattūr performers, and the fact that this name refers to devotional performers (which is what the Mélattūr performers today are), keeping in mind the fact that the word used in reference to Kūchipūdi performance in the Macupalli Kaifiat is Sankīrtana, which again refers to a devotional Bhajan performance (for which the Tarangam performance of the Kūchipūdi tradition alone is an example), the entertainment orientedness of Kūchipūdi tradition should look undoubtedly strange. From this point of view, we may see that the Mélattūr tradition, has preserved the Bhāgavatam type of performance and did not deviate an inch from this. The Kūchipūdi tradition has expanded its repertoire far beyond the limited Bhāgavatam performances.

Prahlāda Charitram is the best example for a Bhāgavatam type story which may have brought the name of Bhāgavatulu to both Kūchipūdi and Mélattūr dancers. Interestingly, this dance drama of Prahlāda Charitram is performed even today in both the traditions. A student of dance should naturally be interested to see closely the dance drama in these two traditions, which are entertainment and devotion oriented, respectively. The book aims at studying the Prahlāda Charitram performances of Kūchipūdi and Mélattūr traditions from this point of view.

REFERENCES

1. The information about Mélattūr tradition is gaining more and more publicity through journalists and academicians talking about it through several platforms.
2. Appa Rao, Vissa, Kūchipūdi: Indian dance, New Delhi, 1954.
3. Ragavan, V., the Vidhi Bhagavatam of Andhra, Vivekanda Patrika, 1981, p. 43.
4. Joga Rao, S.V., Andhra Yaksagana Vangmaya Charitra, Andhra University Publications, Waltair, 1961.
5. Ibid., pp. 176-186, 190-195.
6. Ibid., p. 190.
7. Ibid., pp. 190-191.
8. Ibid., p. 192.
9. Ibid., p. 192.
10. Ibid., p. 193.
11. Ibid., p. 195.

12. Ibid ., p. 195.

13. First page after the inner cover, in Acharya, C.R., 'Kūchipūdi Aradhana Nrityamulu', Eluru, 1969.

14. Ibid., p. 80.

15. Chapeters 7, 8 and 9 pp. 261-413, of Kothari, Sunil, Ph.D Thesis submitted to the M.S. University, Baroda.

16. Ibid., Chapter 10.

17. Ibid., p. 420

18. Ibid., p. 426

19. Ibid., p. 455.

20. Ibid., pp. 455-456.

21. Ramanadam, Chinta, Kūchipūdi school of Yakshagana - literary, traditional and technical perspective, Ph.D Thesis submitted to Andhra University Waltair, 1979, pp. 443-464.

22. Ibid., p. 444.

23. Agraharam, literally means, a row of Brahmin houses. Usually it refers to a village which is exclusively inhabited by Vedic Brahmins, with each house constructed suitably for Vedic rituals. A donation of land for constructing such village was also called donation on Agraharam.

24. Ramanadham, Chinta, Ph.D Thesis, 1979, p. 444.

25. Ibid., pp. 444-445.

26. Ibid., p. 445.

27. Ramanadam, Chinta, Kūchipūdi school of Yakshagāna-literary, traditional and technical perspective, Ph.D Thesis submitted to Andhra University, Waltair, 1979, pp. 461-463.

28. Ragavan, V., 'The Vidhi Bhāgavatam of Andhra', Vivekanda Patrika, 1981, p. 43

29. Vīdhi = street; some scholars feel that Yakshagānam, Vīdhinātakam and Vīdhibhāgavatam are three different art forms. For details on

this discussion, see Joga Rao, S.V. Andhra Yaksagana Vangmaya Charitra, and Published by Andhra University 1961. And also P.S.R. Appa Rao, Kūchipūdi Nrityam, a text book for B.A. Courses of Telugu University.

30. National Book Trust of India, 1980, p. 48.

31. Worship of Vinayaka/Ganesa in the beginning of any activity is believed to be effective in setting off of possible hurdles to that activity and as such Ganesa worship is performed even today by all the devout Hindus for this purpose.

32. For more details, ref. Acharya C.R., "Kūchipūdi Arādhana Nrityamulu", Eluru, 1969.

33. The word Sūtradhāra means the thread holding person. Some people believe that this description refer to the Puppeteer in a puppet show who makes his puppets move by pulling strings. In a Traditional Indian Theatrical Performance, Sūtradhāra is not only the director but also the co-ordinator of the performance.

34. An artist sitting on a side of the stage providing vāchika support and also called as Nattuvanār, according to Prof. Nataraj Ramakrishna. Nattuva is the Telugu word for dancer.

35. Actual details of the traditional Pūrvarangam of Kūchipūdi are not known. The present Pūrvarangam is said to have been reconstructed by late Shri Banda Kanakalingeshwara Rao and others.

36. "Tōdayam" or "Jaya" from the Bhajana Sampradaya of the South is introduced as invocation song followed by "Nāndi Dwipadha" and a "Sabdam" - narration of the story in a nutshell.

37. See Acharya, C.R. "Kūchipūdi Aradhana Nrityamulu", page no. 63, Eluru, 1969.

38. Interview with S. Natarajan, 23rd May, 1996.

39. Interview with S. Natarajan, 23rd May, 1996.

40. Interview with Arudra, 24th May, 1995.

41. Literally it means 'hold' or place or Juncture.

42. There are legends about the female impersonating talents of the Kūchipūdi artist. According to one legend, Vedantam Satyanarayana Sarma was an expert in female impersonation. Once he challenged his wife to recognise him, if she can, when he is in a female constume. Later, once during a ritual in his house, which is supposed to be attended only by women, a woman stayed back even after all the other women left. When his wife enquired with that woman who she was, she turned out to be none other than her own husband.

43. The lyric Bhāmane Satya Bhāmane is quite popular in Telugu households and people talk of the lyric whenever they talk of Kūchipūdi.

44. Quite often this character Madhavi does not appear on the stage. Sūtradhāra himself renders the words of Madhavi.

45. Bhāgavata Méla, Telugu Heritage of Tamil Nadu, by Arudra, in SRUTI, issue no. 22, April 1986, p. 20.

46. Laksmi Narasimha Sastry, Chintalapati gives the date of Narayana Tirta as 1580-1670. Ref. Kūchipūdi Bhāgavatulu, own publications, Tenali, 1983, p. 128.

47. Andhra Yakshagāna Vāngmaya Charita by S.V. Joga Rao, Waltair, 1961, pp. 335-336.

48. Ramanadham Chinta "The Kūchipūdi School of Yakshagāna." A literary traditional and technical perspective, Ph.D Thesis submitted to the Andhra University, Waltair, 1979.

49. Till 1990, only Prahlāda Pattābhishékha Sabdam was sung in the beginning of the Prahlāda play, but Natarajan introduced dancing to the sabdam in the Bhāgavata Méla of Mélattūr.

50. Viranarasimha Rayulu is the son of Tuluva Narasa Nayakudu, the first Tuluva king among the Vijayanagara rulers. Viranarasimha Rayulu ruled for a short period between 1506 A.D and 1509 A.D. Ref. Rayalaseema Telugu "Sasanala Samscritika Adhyanam", by Dr. M. Adinarayana Sastry, Aditya publications, Ananthapuram 1995, p. 116.

51. Munipalli Subrahmanya Kavi is the anthor of these lyrics. He

belongs to the 17 century. Ref. Telugu Sahitya Samiksha by G. Nagayya, Tirupathi.

52. Interview with Dr. Nataraj Ramakrishna, dated 24th August, 1996.

53. Kūchipūdi Aradhana Nrityamulu by C.R. Acharya, Eluru, 1969, pp. 185-186.

54. Though the Nāyaka in all the lyrics is mentioned as Muvva Vénu Gōpāla, a deity in a temple at the village, Muvva of the Krishna District of Andhra Pradesh, which is supposed to be the native place of Kshétrayya the author of these lyrics.

55. Andhra Yakshagāna Vāgmaya Charitra by S.V. Joga Rao, Andhra University Publications, Waltair, 1961, p. 253.

56. Vasakasajja = The Nayika who prepares herself and surroundings and gets ready to receive her beloved.

    Virahotkanthita = The Nāyika who suffers because she is seperated from her beloved.

    Swadhinabhartrika = The Nāyika whose beloved is devoted to her and who has risen to her expectation.

    Kalahantarita = The Nāyika who fights with her beloved and then regrets her behaviour being filled with remorse and repentance.

    Khanditha = The Nāyika who is enraged with her beloved for being unfaithful to her.

    Vipralabdha = The Nāyika who is deceived by the lord.

    Proshitabhartrika = The Nāyika who suffers pangs of seperation when her beloved is away from her. She has not fought with him.

    Abhisarika = The Nāyika who is uncaring for and against all odds goes out to meet her beloved.

57. Telugu Sahitya Samiksha, vol. no. 2 by G. Nagayya own publication, Tirupati.

58. The word 'Sāttvika' stems from the Sanskrit word 'Sattva' and it relates to the expressions comming fourth from a dancer as a

result of a particular emotion he/she experiences within. It relates to the inner psychological state and mental feelings which when expressed create the relevant mood or emotion in others. Sāttvika Abhinaya is that aspect of Abhinaya which contributes towards the effective creation or Rasa in the spectator.

59. Jāvali is an erotic lyric usually performed in medium or fast rhythm, unlike the Kshetrayya Padams which are sung in slow tempo.

60. Interview with Ramanadham. C., 26th Novermber, 1996.

61. Triputa Talam (Tisra Jati Triputa Talam) has Laghu, and 2 drutams. In Tisra Jati, Laghu have three beats and each drutam have two beats, i.e., 3+2+2=7.

62. Interview with Prof. Nataraj Ramakrishna, 6th June, 1996.

63. Interview with Prof. Nataraj Ramakrishna, 6th June, 1996.

64. Interview with Prof. Nataraj Ramakrishna dated 10th September 1996.

65. "Studies in the history of the third dynasty of Vijayanagara" by Dr. N. Venkata Ramaiah garu, Appendix-c, pages 462-463. As cited in Kūchipūdi Bhāgavatulu by Laxminarasimha Sastry Chintalapati, own publication, Tenali, 1983, p. 28.

66. Pagativésalu are small mock theatrical performances of humorous nature, performed usually by folk artists on the streets during day time.

2

Sources and Significance of Prahlāda Story in Kūchipūdi and Mélattūr Dance Traditions

Prahlāda Vijayamu of the Kūchipūdi and Prahlāda Charitram of the Mélattūr traditions are both in the genre of Yakhagānam performances of the story of Prahlāda, a devotee of Lord Vishnu. Lord Vishnu, according to Hindu mythology, is one of the three almighty Gods, Bramha and Siva being the other two. Bramha is the creator, Vishnu, the sustainer and Siva dissolves the universe. Lord Vishnu incarnates on the earth from time to time to kill the demons that torment the universe. The story of Prahlāda is also known as the story of Lord Narasimha, who is one such incarnation of Lord Vishnu in the form of a lion-headed human. In this story, Lord Vishnu emerges from a pillar and kills Hiranyakasipu, father of Prahlāda, to protect his devotee Prahlāda.

According to Hindu mythology, the incidents in this story took place during the mythological time period called "Kritayuga". During this time, Lord Vishnu killed Hiranyāksha, brother of Hiranyakasipu, in order to save the earth. In this story Vishnu kills Hiranyāksha in his incarnation as "Varāha", the wild boar who brings earth out of water on his two tusks.

Hiranyakasipu wants to avenge the killing of his brother and thus becomes the sworn enemy of Vishnu. But ironically he begets a son called Prahlāda who is a staunch devotee of Lord Vishnu. Hiranyakasipu fails in his attempts to reform his son and make him give up his devotion for Lord Vishnu despite getting him educated by the family gurus. Hiranyakasipu tortures his son by throwing him into boiling oil, trampling him under the feet of an elephant, throwing him down from a high mountain, etc., but the boy comes out unaffected through these ordeals as Lord Vishnu protects him all through. Hiranyakasipu in desperation, asks his son to show him Lord Vishnu in the pillar in front of him, if Vishnu was really all pervading as the boy had claimed. Prahlāda advises his father Hiranyakasipu to call the Lord himself and assures him that he is present even in the pillar. Hiranyakasipu shouts loudly challenging Lord Vishnu to come out if he were really present in the pillar. The pillar breaks open with a huge sound and Narasimha the Lion-man crashes out of it, stoops over Hiranyakasipu and kills him. After this, Lord Vishnu in the form of Narasimha cools down and blesses Prahlāda to rule over the earth for aeons and ultimately get liberated and reach Vishnulōka (the world of Lord Vishnu). This is the common structure of the Prahlāda Narasimha story of all the puranās.

One of the versions argues that Hiranyakasipu did penance to please Lord Bramha and obtained a boon that he shall not be killed by any human being or an animal or a terrestrial creature or celestial beings, neither during the day nor during the night, neither inside the house nor outside the house. Lord Vishnu incarnated as half animal and half human semi-divine form and killed Hiranyakasipu at sun set on the threshold of his house[1] so that the boon does not protect the demon.

According to the devotional version of the story Hiranyakasipu and Hiranyāksha, in their earlier forms (before incarnating as demons) were the doorkeepers of Lord Vishnu's abode, 'Vaikuntha'. Once they insulted the sages called Sanaka, Sanandana, and Sanatkumāra by disallowing them into Vaikuntha. The sages, angry at the behaviour of Jaya and Vijaya, the doorkeepers, cursed them to take birth on the earth. The doorkeepers were shocked and depressed by the sudden turn of events and begged for reprieval from the curse. Lord Vishnu intervenes at this juncture and offers them a choice between two schemes of reprieval from the curse. According to one, Jaya and Vijaya shall be born as devotees of Lord Vishnu and come back to Vaikuntha after seven such births as devotees and according to the second they shall be born as demons who are sworn enemies of Lord Vishnu and they shall come back to Vaikunta after three such births as demons. Jaya and Vijaya chose the second as it means a shorter separation from Lord Vishnu and Vaikuntha than the first. As a result, they took birth as Hiranyakasipu and Hiranyāksha in Kritayuga, Rāvana and Kumbhakarna in Trétayuga and as Sisupāla and Dantavaktra in Dwaparayuga[2]. Srimad Bhāgavata is the most important source for this devotional version in which Hiranyakasipu and Hiranyāksha engage in 'Vaira Bhakti' (devotion in the form of enmity) with Lord Vishnu. According to this version, both Hiranyakasipu and Prahlāda are Vishnu's devotees, of different kinds, one in the form of an enemy, the other completely surrendered to the Lord.

Both Kūchipūdi and Mélattūr Yakshagānam performances follow this version of the story, which is, in fact, a result of the impact of the Bhakti movement. This story is one of the most prominent stories of the Bhāgavata Purānam. It is considered as a story of the incarnation of Lord Vishnu, of Dévāsura sangramas (God-Demon battles), and the most exemplary ancient devotees of Lord Vishnu.

Thus, the significance of Prahlāda Charitra Nātakam in the repertoire of both these dance forms (both are called as Bhāgavata traditions) lies in its being *(a)* a story from the Bhāgavata Purāna, *(b)* a story of the Bhāgavatārs (devotees), and *(c)* a story with a Bhāgavata (devotional) approach.

This story appears in the Agnipurāna, Vishnu Purāna, Rāvana Purāna, Matsya Purāna, Devi Bhāgavata and Sthala Puranās, such as Nrisimha Puranās. Different Puranās give different versions of the Narasimha story. In fact, the differences between these versions are not significant. There are minor differences in details, such as the name of the wife of the Hiranyakasipu, etc. The most prominently used name is Līlāvati but in some Puranās the name is "Kayādhu". The names of the teachers of Prahlāda also vary. But the main story line of the Narasimha story in all the Puranās is almost the same.

The Puranic literature on Narasimha cult is very rich. In this literature, there are several interpretations of the concept of the Narasimha. But the spread of the cult of Narasimha is not limited to the puranic classical tradition alone. This cult is widespread among folk and tribal traditions also. For example, there is a vibrant tribal tradition of Narasimha worship among the 'Chenchūs' of the southern Andhra Pradesh. This tradition is centred on a shrine of Narasimha called Ahōbilam in the Kurnool district of Andhra Pradesh. According to Chenchu tradition of Narasimha worship, Narasimha fell in love with a Chenchu girl called 'Chenchu Lakshmi' and the girl and her community accepted Narsimha after he passed all the tests in the skills of forest life. After Narasimha established his skills, Chenchu Lakshmi married Narasimha and thus, Narasimha became the son-in-law / brother-in-law of the Chenchu community. All the Chenchus of Andhra Pradesh worship Narasimha from this point of view. There are folk epic songs narrating this version of Narasimha story. This story forms a part of several Chenchu tribal dance songs and other Chenchu lyrics. This story gained popularity among the rural as well as the urban people of Andhra Pradesh. Dramas and films based on this story became popular among the Telugu public. The puranic version of the Narasimha story and this tribal version of it got intertwined without any contradiction. But both the Kūchipūdi and Mélattūr texts of Narasimha story (Prahlāda Charitra) consciously include only the Puranic version of the story, and not the tribal version.

Lord Narasimha is one of the most popular deities of the Hindu mythology and the temples and cult of worship of this deity is widely prevalent throughout South India, especially in Andhra Pradesh. In fact, the Mélattūr Prahlāda Nātakam performance is associated with the worship of Narasimha and the Narasimha temple of the Mélattūr town. This association is so sacred and strictly maintained that the Mélattūr Bhāgavata Méla Nātakam team does not perform the Nātakam anywhere else other than in the premises of the local Narasimha temple of the Mélattūr town.

The cult of Narasimha is so widespread among the Telugu people that the word Narasimha appears in personal and family names and names of the places from a long time. For several families belonging to different communities ranging from Dvijas (Brahmins, Kshatriyas and Vysyas) to the Dalit communities, Narasimha is a family deity (the worship of a family deity is a strong, sacred and inviolable custom). There are several ritual requirements of the worship of family deity and people following this tradition who believe that the family deity must be worshipped so that he takes care of the family and protects them from troubles and destruction. The family deity is to be worshiped on all-important ritual occasions. An annual ritual exclusively devoted to the worship of the family deity and an annual visit to the shrine of the family deity is a must.

It is interesting to see that among all the Avatārās of Vishnu believed to have incarnated during the early period of Kritayuga, only Narasimha Avatara has acquired a place in the traditions of the temple iconography, magic and supernatural practices. In this respect, Narasimha is closely comparable to Sakti, Hanuman and Ganésa.

There are several shrines where the principal deity is Narasimha. Interestingly most of these shrines are hill shrines with a tradition of worship built around each of them. Mādabhūshini Narasimhāchārya, a historian, has extensively researched on the history of the cult of Narasimha in Andhra Pradesh from 11th century A.D. to 17th Century A.D. In a book with the same title he discusses the origin of the cult of Narasimha and the cult and history of the different centers of the Narasimha worship in all the three regions (Rayalaseema, Coastal Andhra and Telangana) of Andhra Pradesh. Rituals and festivals of Narasimha cult, as mentioned in the inscriptions and iconography of the cult, a map of selected centres of Narasimha worship in Andhra Pradesh, is reproduced in this book (Figure-I).

Thus, we can see that the cult of Narasimha has had at least a history of a thousand years. And this history was reflected in the classical literature, folk songs and theatrical and dance forms for a long time. The significance of the Narasimha story in Kūchipūdi and Mélattūr traditions should be seen from the perspective of this historical significance.

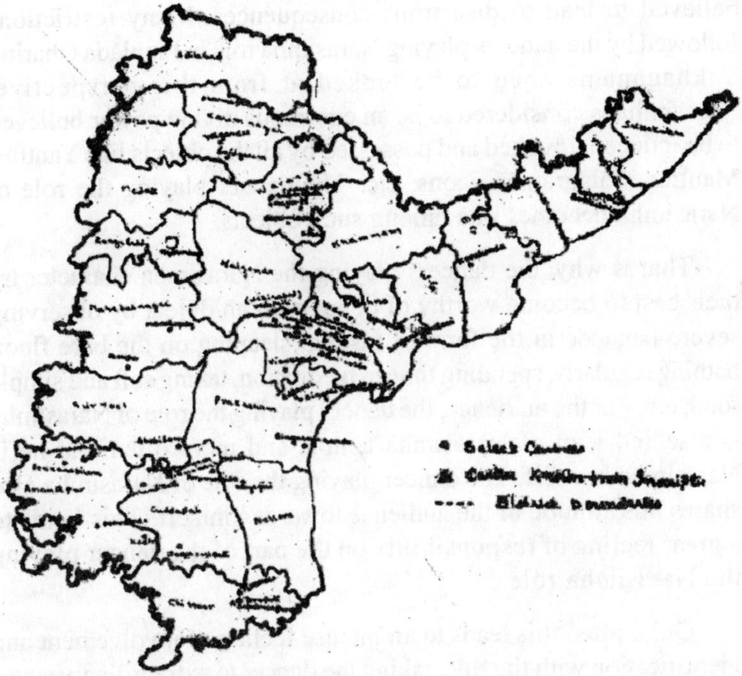

Figure-I: Map of Selected Centres of Narasimha. Reproduced from Mādabhūshini Narasimhachārya's Book.

There are Yantras (symbolic drawings used for magical practices) of Narasimha, and Salagramas (precious or fossilised stones) that are believed to possess the power of Narasimha. Various iconographical figures of Narasimha are worshipped, both at the household and temple levels. There are mantras (hymns, magical syllable sequences or spells) of Narasimha discussed in Mantra Sastra (the science of the power of spells). Narasimha upāsana (devout spiritual practices centred round the concept of Narasimha) is also vibrantly prevalent among spiritual practitioners. The worship of yantrās, sālagrāmās, icons, mantras, etc., involves a severe life of restriction with regard to the sanctity and piousness. Such practices are believed to be effective in giving supernatural powers to their practitioners. Violation of the rules of these practices is believed to lead to disastrous consequences. Many restrictions followed by the dancers playing Narasimha role in Prahlāda Charitra Yakhagānams need to be looked at from this perspective. Narasimha is considered to be an enormous divine power believed to be induced, invoked and possessed by all the objects like Yantrās, Mantras, Sālagrāmās, icons, etc. The dancer playing the role of Narasimha becomes one among such objects.

That is why, the dancers playing the Narasimha character try their best to become worthy of being such an object by observing severe penance in the form of fasting, sleeping on the bare floor, bathing regularly, spending time in meditation, taking soft and simple food, etc. For the audience, the dancer playing the role of Narasimha is a sacred icon of Narasimha temple and more often that he is Narasimha himself. The dancer playing the role of Narasimha also shares this attitude of the audience towards himself. This leads to a great feeling of responsibility on the part of the dancer playing the Narasimha role.

Quite often this leads to an intense feeling of involvement and identification with the role, taking the dancer to extraordinary states of ecstasy. This is considered to be the possession of the dancer by the spirit of Narasimha. Both the audience and dancer share this feeling. This is said to have lead to several problems on the stage like the dancer playing the Narasimha role actually killing the dancer playing the role of Hiranyakasipu or the Narasimha character going berserk on the stage and after a long uncontrollable ferocious movements the dancer falling down unconscious on the stage, etc. Even today in the Mélattūr Nātakam the Narasimha role player is tied with a cloth and is clipped on either side by four or five stage assistants (Plate-II). This indicates the caution on the part of the team to prevent any possible repetition of the problem described above. Kūchipūdi performers of Prahlāda Charitra Nātakam recount that a similar practice of chaining Narasimha used to exist even in Kūchipūdi tradition[3]. They even recount a few incidents which lead to these arrangements. According to them, once two brothers playing the roles of Hiranyakasipu and Narasimha got into a state of trance and the Narasimha character killed the other who was playing the Hiranyakasipu character. From then on the team began to chain the Narasimha character to avoid any such mishaps. But in course of time the team realised that the involvement of the dancers is gradually decreasing and, therefore, such precautions are not really necessary.[4]

Plate-II: The Mélattūr Performance Assistants Tying the Narasimha Dancer before the Performance Begins.

In this context, another noteworthy aspect of both the Kūchipūdi and Mélattūr forms is the use of mask for the depiction of Narasimha character. Mask is not a dominant feature in Kūchipūdi and Mēlattūr. Kūchipūdi Bhāgavatārs used very few masks. One of them is the mask of Ganésa, which they use in Vināyaka Pravésham, in the beginning of all the Kūchipūdi dance dramas. The performer wearing the Ganésa mask comes on to the stage and dances to the lyrics being sung by Sūtradhāra/ Nattuvanār (Plate-II) paying obeisance to Vināyaka. This is one of the items common to both the Kūchipūdi and Mélattūr performances (Plate-III). Mélattūr team uses masks even for the Rākshasa (demon) characters (Plate-IV). For the Mélattūr team the Narasimha mask (Plate-V) is more than a mere costume. They preserve and worship the mask as a sacred ritual item, as an icon (Plate-VI). The Kūchipūdi team, contrastingly, does not maintain such an iconic attitude towards Narasimha mask (Plate-VII). Both the Kūchipūdi and Mélattūr Narasimha masks are influenced by the temple icons of Narasimha.

Both the audience and dancers are heavily influenced by the figures of Narasimha found in the temples (Plate-VIII). Mādabhūshini Narasimhācharya[5] in his book, mentioned above, discusses the different forms of Narasimha found in temple sculptures. They are:

(*a*) Yōgānanda Lakshmi Narasimha (Narasimha in yoga posture with Lakshmi),

(*b*) Varāha Lakshmī Narashima,

(*c*) Prahlādānugraha Murti (Narasimha blessing Prahlāda),

(*d*) Narasimha and Chencheta, and

(*e*) Narasimha in Hari-Hara aspects.

Plate-III: The Vināyaka Dancer of Mélattūr Prahlāda Nātakam with Mask.

Plate-IV: The Rākshasa Dancers of Mélattūr Prahlāda Nātakam with Masks.

Plate-V: Narasimha Mask of Mélattūr Prahlāda Nātakam placed among other Icons of Worship, ready to be taken out in a procession.

Plate-VI: The Narasimha Mask of Mélattūr Prahlāda Nātakam is preserved here in this wooden enclosure.

Plate-VII: Narasimha Mask once used by Kūchipūdi team taken from video recording of Prahlāda Nātakam Performance (Source: J. Anuradha, University of Hyderabad).

Plate-VIII: The Narasimha Icon (with his consorts) worshipped in the Varada Raja Perumal Temple, Mélattūr.

A general noteworthy feature of the sculptures of Narasimha is that in early medieval representation the lion face was natural and later on it got stylized. According to the examples available, the various forms of Narasimha[6] are given below:

S. No.	*Types of Sculpture*	*Total Number of Available Sculptures*
1.	Kevala Narasimha (standing)	15
2.	Girija Narasimha (seated)	37
3.	Yoga Narasimha	40
4.	Sthauna Narasimha	33
5.	Yanaka Narasimha	2
6.	Lakshmi Narasimha	34
7.	Yogananda Lakshmi Narasimha	1
8.	Varaha Lakshmi Narasimha	2
9.	Prahaladanugraha Murti	3
10.	Narasimha and Cencheta (Narasimha wooing chencheta)	3
11.	Narasimha in Hari-Hara aspects and Tandava (Nritta)	1
12.	Narasimha	2

He talks even about the Nava Narasimhas[7]. They are:

1. Ugra (angry)
2. Vira (Fighting)
3. MahVishnu (Lakshmi Narasimha)
4. Jvalanta (emitting flames of fire)
5. Sarvoatomukham (with a number of faces)
6. Narisimham (ordinary Narasimha)
7. Bhisanam (frightful)
8. Bhadram (adorable) and
9. Mrityor-mrityu (the killer of death).

As one can easily imagine, the costume (āhārya) and dance postures of the dancers are influenced by these images gained from visiting the temples of Narasimha with these figures (Plates-IX & X).

Plate-IX

(a) Kevala Narasimha-Panchaviras, Kondamotu, Guntur District

(*b*) Yoga Narasimha, Vaddemanu – Mahabubnagar District

(*c*) Yoga Narasimha, Lower Ahobilam

Plate-X

(*a*) Lakshmi Narasimha – (Nava Narasimhas), Upper Ahobilam

(*b*) Yogananda Lakshmi Narasimha – Lower Ahobilam

(c) Sthana Narasimha–Vidarana (Nava Narasimhas) Lower Ahobilam

Mādabhūsini Narasimhāchārya in his book cited the above details along with the rituals and festivals centred round Narasimha. According to his description, the rituals and festivals are as old as the Narasimha cult itself. The most important of these rituals is Narasimha Jayanti. This falls on the fourteenth day of the bright half of the month of Vaisākha. He further mentions that an inscription dated 1287 A.D. mentions the celebration of Narasimha Jayanti at the Simhāchalam Temple near Visakhapatnam. He also mentions another inscription of 1512 A.D., which talks of Narasimha Jayanti celebration at Srinivāsapuram, a suburb of Tirupati (This information is very important for the study of Mélattūr performance of Prahlāda Nātakam). The Mélattūr family also performs this dance drama, that too on Narasimha Jayanti and only in the premises of the Narasimha temple of Mélattūr. Performance of dance dramas in the premises of temples is also an ancient tradition. Mādabhūsini Narasimhāchārya talks of the Dévadāsi tradition prevailing in Narasimha temples. However, in the performances of Mēlattūr, the Prahlāda Nātakam has nothing to do with the Dévadāsi tradition.

But the performance of dance-drama of Prahlāda Nātakam is part of the worship offered to the Lord Narasimha, the deity in the temple at Mēlattūr. Though the Kūchipūdi Prahlāda Nātakam is not part of Narasimha Jayanthi festival, nor is restricted to the premises of any Narasimha temple, the Prahlāda Nātakam even within the Kūchipūdi tradition is definitely related to the Narasimha cult in Andhra Pradesh. A famous centre of Narasimha cult is Mangalagiri, in the neighbourhood of the famous town Guntur. This is very close to Kūchipūdi and the cult of Narasimha is also one of the significant cults prevalent in Kūchipūdi and the neighbouring villages.

As has already been mentioned, Narasimha is one of the Dasāvatāras, the ten incarnations, of Lord Vishnu. With regard to the concept of Narasimha Avatāra, Mādabhūsini Narasimhāchārya says that the concept of Narasimha is as old as the Védas. He says the earliest reference to Narasimha is given in the Taittiriya Aranyaka, and in this Aranyaka the almighty is described as "Possessing sharp claws and fangs." Then he goes on to quote Mahānārāyana Upanishad and Narasimha Uttaratāpanīya Upanishad. The historical dates of these Upanishads are not clear. But Narasimhāchārya's reference to the mentioning of Narasimha in Mahabharata is important.

Traditions regarding the number of Avatārās vary; in some it is 39 and in some others it is 22; while some books mention 19 Avatārās. The most popular concept is that of ten Avatārās. Vaisnava literature classifies Avatārās into three kinds namely: *(a)* Purnavatara (complete incarnation), *(b)* Amsāvatara (incarnation of a portion of the power of the divine being), *(c)* Avésa (partial incarnation of a more or less temporary character).

There are several esoteric interpretations of the concept of Narasimha. Madabhusini Narasimhacharya quotes one such interpretation by Prof. Vasudéva S Agravala. The interpretation is as follows:

> Narasimha is a type of purushāpasu, in which the lion being an animal of the forest is the symbol of the unharnessed energy of the divine-paraméshthi, who is described as forest

(Brahma-vana). That power of universal comes to the level of Matter and creates the Man-lion form. It deals with Hiranyakasyapa or region of Prakrit. Kasyapa literally means a cushion or seat of gold or Hiranya, Hiranya is the principle of Prāna, which descends to the level of matter. Hiranya is PurUshā and Kasipu is Prakriti. Both of them combine in the golden egg, in which Prakriti offers herself as a saint for the divine Hiranyagarbha. The idea of the legend is that Hiranya Kasyapa how so ever powerful in the three worlds succumbs to the might of Narasimha.

But this esoteric interpretation is not relevant for the Mélattūr or Kūchipūdi performances because neither the performers nor the audience of these performances are aware of these interpretations.

In fact, Narasimha worship is especially significant for the Vaishnavaite tradition, especially the Visishtadvaita tradition. Interestingly neither the Kūchipūdi performers nor the Mélattūr performers are Vaishnavaites. Both these dancing families belong to the Smartha Brahmin sect which is an advaitic sect. But within the advaitic sect there is no negation of the worship of almighty in the form of Vishnu or one of his avatarās. Thus, the prevalence of Narasimha cult among the Mélattūr and Kūchipūdi families is not against the advaitic tradition of these families. Interviews with both the Kūchipūdi and Mélattūr performers have revealed that neither of these families is seriously trained nor do they have a serious commitment for advaitic/védantic interpretation of the stories they perform.

ARTISTIC ASPECTS OF PRAHLĀDA CHARITRA STORY

From both the literary or performance arts point of view, the story of Prahlāda Charitra must have possessed several attractive features. Otherwise, it could not have attracted the attention of theatrical, dance and poetic artistes in so many languages and regions of India.

The story has gripping drama in the form of an irreconcilable conflict between a father and his son in terms of their goals of life, personalities and worldviews. The drama is rooted in the fact that the only son who is the heir to the crown is the object of his father's concentrated affection. But the son is a staunch devotee of the arch enemy of his father. For Hiranyakasipu, the father, his enmity towards Lord Vishnu is the goal of his life. Prahlāda's devotion to Lord Vishnu is the essence and meaning of his personality, life and existence. This drama has its narrative beginning in two incidents. The first is killing of Hiranyāksha, brother of Hiranyakasipu by Lord Vishnu. The second is the asylum (shelter) given by sage Narada, the great devotee of Lord Vishnu, to the wife of Hiranyakasipu (Līlāvati according to the Kūchipūdi and Mélattūr texts) while she had Prahlāda in her womb. Narada rescued her from Indra who kidnapped her while Hiranyakasipu was away for his penance.

Sage Narada influenced Prahlāda right in his prenatal days to become a staunch devotee of Lord Vishnu. This act of Narada is explained as the game of nature which took care to sow the seeds of countering the plans of Hiranyakasipu who was striving to achieve immortality. The boon of immortality given by Brahma to Hiranyakasipu apparently appears to have exhausted all the possibilities of death. But when Hiranyakasipu ultimately gets killed by a man-lion, who is neither a human being nor an animal, during the dusk, which is neither day nor night, on the threshold of his house, which is neither inside nor outside the house, with the nails of the man-lion, which is no weapon, the deficiencies in the possibility of death as imagined by Hiranyakasipu are exposed. This makes it clear how nature always has a room to implement its law of death even when people try to leave no such chance to it. This ending of the story gives an interesting resolution to the entire drama of the father-son conflict. Hiranyakasipu who seeks to achieve immortality is awarded death, whereas Prahlāda who never bothered about his death is blessed with a long life lasting aeons. Hiranyakasipu and Prahlāda are depicted as personifications or allegories of arrogance and surrender towards the sustainer of nature, Lord Vishnu, respectively.

There are several other interesting oppositions between Hiranyakasipu and Prahlāda in this story. Hiranyakasipu is violent, crude, experienced, and power hungry person. Prahlāda is non-violent, polite and young. Throughout the story, the violence, power and experience of Hiranyakasipu repeatedly gets defeated in the hands of the non-violent, polite, soft, young and seemingly powerless Prahlāda. This happens without any volition on the part of Prahlāda. The power protecting Prahlāda is the grace of Lord Vishnu, which is the result of Prahlāda's complete surrender to the Lord.

Thus, more than Prahlāda himself, his devotion to Lord Vishnu is the victor in this story and the entire story ends on the note of victory of devotion. Bhakti, devotion, is thus the main theme and message, and is central to the emotion of the story of Prahlāda Charitra. Hence, from a rasa point of view, the story of Prahlāda Charitra is replete with Bhakti rasa.

Though the Bhakti rasa is angi (central) rasa, there are several anga (component) rasas of the story like Bhayānaka (fear), Vātsalya (affection towards a child or a younger person), Hāsya (humour), etc. From a dancer's point of view it is this aspect of the story that is significant because ultimately Nātya is the enactment of rasa to help its audiences relish the same.

Especially, in dance-drama form, such as the Kūchipūdi and Mélattūr Bhāgavata Méla, the rasa depiction has a narrative component. More than the depiction of individual rasas, the enactment of the rasa combinations and movement of the narrative from one rasa to the other becomes important. The story begins with the Roudra (anger) rasa but the Alambana Vibhāva (the holder of the rasa) is the villain of the story. As is well known, the last important episode of the Prahlāda Nātakam embodies the Roudra rasam but the holder of the emotion this time is Narasimha, the protector of the hero of the story Prahlāda. These two episodes with Roudra rasam as the mainstay are connected in between by the other episodes for playing the other rasas. For example, in response to Hiranyakasipu's anger Līlāvati tries to cool him down and this episode is full of Santa (calmness) rasa or Karuna (sympathy) rasa. The episode is designed to be unusually long, probably to affect a balance between the anger and its pacification.

In response to Līlāvati's calmness, Hiranyakasipu talks about his valour and might. From the rasa point of view, this is Vīra. Another important rasa (especially in the Mélattūr version) is Hāsya (Humour), which occurs in the episode of Rākshasas (demons) searching for Vishnu on the orders of Hiranyakasipu and the episode of Prahlāda being trained into the Rākshasa tradition by the gurus Chanda and Amarka. Both Chanda and Amarka are depicted as foolish teachers suffering in the hands of the adamant devotee of Lord Vishnu. Thus, the different rasas intersperse the central Bhakti rasa, which runs through all the episodes.

LITERARY SOURCES

Madabhushini Narasimhacharya mentions the following Telugu literary sources of story of the Narasimha in his research work. Following are the Telugu literary sources giving information on the cult of Narasimha in Andhra Pradesh:

1. NARASIMHA PURANA OF ERRAPRAGADA

Errapragada, one of the famous kavitraya (Trinity) who lived during 1324-1349 A.D. wrote Lakshmi Narasimha Purāna and dedicated it to Lord Ahōbila Narasimha Swamy. The fifth chapter of the Purāna describes the importance of Ahōbilam Kshétra and its God. In this Purāna the poet mentions 'Simhādri' as a place of pilgrimage.

2. PADMAPURANA OF MADIKISINGANA

Madikisingana wrote Padma purāna (Uttara Khanda) in the year 1420 A.D. It is stated in his work that the noble minister, Kesana of Muppa Bhupala of Ramgiri (Karimnagar District) had given gifts for maintaining 'annasastram' (feeding house) and conducting the 'Utsavas' (celebrations) to God Narasimha of Dharmapuri. In the seventh canto of the Purāna, the legend of the birth of Narasimha and the destruction of the demon, Hiranyakasipu is given.

3. BHAGAVATAM OF BAMMERA POTANA

Bammera Potana, the famous Telugu Poet, lived during 1400-1470

A.D. and hailed from Warangal district. He translated the Sanskrit Bhāgavatam into Telugu. The birth of Narasimha and the destruction of the demon, Hiranyakasipu are described in the Saptama Skandha of the book.

4. SIMHASANA DVATRIMSIKA OF KORAVI GOPA RAJU

Koravi Gopa Raju, who lived during 1430-1490 A.D., wrote 'Simhasanadvatrimsika', in which he mentions that Hari and Kara came to Dharmapuri as Narasimha and Ramesvara. Besides, the poet describes Dharmapuri in the five stanzas in the 21 picture story.

5. NRISIMHA PURANA OF HARIBHATTU

Haribhattu, who lived around 1530 A.D., wrote Nrisimha Purana (uttara bhagam) in champu kavya style, just as Errana had written the first part of Narasimha Purāna earlier.

6. SANKIRTANAS of TALLAPAKA POETS

The Tāllapāka poets, such as Annamayya (1408-1507 A.D.) and Peda Tirumalacharyulu (1460-1547 A.D.) wrote a number of 'Sankirtanas' (devotional songs) in favour of Ahobila Narasimha. It is stated that the third Tāllapāka poet, Tirumalacharyulu (1485-1550 A.D.) had consecrated the idol of Narasimha at the Hunumān shrine in Tirupati. It is stated that Annmayya visited the Ahōbilam temple and sang the glory of God Narasimha. It is attested by two copper plates of Annamacharya's kīrtanas, which are found at Ahōbilam. He praised the Lord of upper Ahōbilam as the boon giver.

7. VISHNU PURANA OF VENNELAKANTI SURANNA

Vennelakanti Suranna, who lived in the first part of the 16th century A.D., had translated the Sanskrit Vishnu Purana into Telugu named 'Andhra Sri Vishnu Purānam' describing the incarnation of Lord Vishnu. The legend of Prahlāda, the birth of Lord Narasimha and the destruction of Hiranyakasipu are narrated in this Purana.

8. GHATIKACHALA MAHATMYAM OF TENALIRAMA-KRISHNA

It is believed that Tenali Rama Krishna lived during the last part of the 16th century A.D. He wrote Sri Ghatikachala Mahatmyamu wherein he described God Narasimha at Ghatikachala (North Arcot district of Tamil Nadu).

9. GARUDACHALA VILASAMU OF OBAYAMANTRI

Obayamantri, who lived in the 17th century, wrote Garudachala Vilasamu, a very popular Yakshagāna, describing the marriage of God Narasimha of Ahōbilam with a girl belonging to the Chenchu tribe.

10. THE DEVOTIONAL SONGS OF SIVA NARAYANA TIRTULU

Siva Narayana Tirtulu, who lived in the 17th century, wrote devotional songs on Sobhanadri Sri Narasimha (Agiripalli of Krishna District) and Vedadri Narasimha (Krishna district).

11. PRAHLĀDA VIJAYAMU OF VIJAYA RAGHAVA NAYAKA

Vijayaraghava Nayaka, who ruled Tanjore from 1633 to 1673 A.D., wrote Prahlāda Charitram in Telugu.

Following are the Telugu literary sources, which make passing references to the cult of Narasimha in Andhra Pradesh.

1. PRATAPA CHARITRA OF EKAMRANATHA

It is mentioned that Ahobilam, Mangalagiri, Simhachalam, Srikurmam and other temples enjoyed the patronage from the treasury of Kakatiya Prataparudra II (1290-1323 A.D.).

2. HARIVAMSAM (UTTARA BHAGAM) OF ERRAPRAGADA

Errapragada, wrote Harivamsam (uttara bhagam). It is stated in the preface that Vema Reddi (1324-1353 A.D.) had built the steps to the upper Ahōbilam.

3. SIMHAGIRI VACHANAMULU OF KRISHNAMACHARYA

The Pratapa Charitra mentions that Krishnamacharya was appointed as an officer of fifty villages in Kanakagirisima. He wrote 'Simhagiri

Vachanamulu' in prose and happened to be the first man to initiate prose writing in Telugu in the fourteenth century A.D.

4. *NARAYANA SATAKAMU OF BAMMERA POTANA*

Narayana Satakamu is attributed to Bammera Potana, a famous Telugu poet, in which he implored the God "Dharmapuri Lakshminatha Narayana", who is none other than Narasimha, as there is no other temple of Vishnu of that time except the temple of Narasimha.

5. *BHOJARAJIYAM OF ANANTAMATYA*

Anantamatya, who lived in the fifteenth century A.D. dedicated his work, named 'Bhojarajiyam[5] to God Ahōbilam Narasimha

6. *KASIKHANDAM, BHIMESVARAPURANAM AND SIMHADRI TIRUNALLU OF SRINATHA*

The popular Telugu romantic poet, Srinatha wrote Sri Kasikhandam and dedicated it to King Virabhadra Reddy of Rajamahendravaram in 1440 A.D. as was stated in the 'Pithika'. In it, God Vedadri Narasimha and Ahobilam are mentioned.

In his other work 'Bhimesvara Purānam', the poet refers to 'Simhadri Lakshmi Narasimha', while describing the pilgrimages of Vyasa Maharshi.

This poet also describes a festive gathering at the Kshétra (Sacred Place) of Simhachalam in his work, entitled 'Simhadri Tirunallu'.

7. *CHITRA BHAARATAMU OF CHARIGONDA DHARMANNA*

Charigonda Dharmanna who belonged to the village of Charigonda in Mahabubnagar district is said to have written 'Chitra Bhāratamu' during 1503-1512 A.D. It is mentioned clearly that the poet went to Dharmapuri and described the greatness of the God in his work. Besides, it is stated that Enumulapalli Peddana who was a minister of Shitabhan of Warangal was a great devotee of God Narasimha of Dharmapuri.

8. AMUKTAMALYADA OF SRIKRISHNADEVARAYA

Krishnadevaraya (1509-1529 A.D.), the great poet-king of Vijayanagara, makes a passing reference to the fair (Tirunal) of Simhachala Swami (Lord of Simhachalam) at Simhachalam in his work 'Āmkutamālyada'. In it, he mentions that even 'dẹvas' (gods) also participated in the fair.

9. KALA PURNODAYAM OF PINGALI SURANA

The renowned Telugu Poet, Pingali Surana, who lived about 1560 A.D., refers to Dharmapuri (Karimnagar district) on the bank of river Godavari. Simhachaladhisa and Srimand Ahobila Swami in his great classic 'kālapūrnōdayam' while describing the pilgrimage of Manikhandhara.

10. THE YAKSHAGĀNAMU OF KANDUKURI RUDRAYYA

Kandukuri Rudrayya, who lived during 1490-1570 A.D., wrote a 'Yakshagāna', which is the first of its kind in Telugu language. In his work, the poet referred to God Narasimha as Adimurti Narasimha.

11. VIJAYAVILASAMU OF CHEMAKURA VENKATA KAVI

The poet Chemakura Venkata Kavi wrote 'Vijayavilāsamu' and dedicated it to Raghunathabhupala (1600-1631 A.D.). The poet, narrating the pilgrimage made by Arjuna, a popular hero of Hindu mythology, refers to his homage to God Narasimha of Antarvedi (East Godavari district) and his dip at the confluence there.

PRAHLĀDA CHARITRA IN TELUGU LITERATURE-POTANA'S BHAGAVATAM-POPULAR SOURCES

Though Prahlāda Charitram has been dealt with even during 14th Century in books like Yerrana's Nrisimha Purānam, the work that influenced the later writers the most is Potana's Bhāgavatam composed in the 15th century. Potana's Bhāgavatam is probably the only classical work, which has been popular in the households of the Telugu people for generations. The traditional Telugu people as a part of their day-to-day activities recite different episodes of his

Bhāgavatam. For example, the Gajéndra Mōksham (the liberation of an elephant from the clutches of a crocodile) episode is sung during the early morning bath at the village tank/river/backyard/well, etc. Similarly, the Vāman Avatāram, Rukhminīkalyānam, Prahlāda Charitram and other episodes are sung in the daily routine in Telugu families. Many verses from the Prahlāda Charitram of Potana are popular with Telugu people. It is important to note that the Telugu audience's view of Prahlāda Charitram is governed by Potana's compositions, which they are conversant with. Most of the narrative art performances like Purānakālakshépam (Purāna recital in temples) and Hirakata Kālakshépam (a dance-song and recital performance form) deal with the Prahlāda Charitram theme. Prahlāda Charitram is narrated quite often with the help of Pothana's compositions only. Telugu films on Prahlāda Charitram have used Pothana's compositions extensively in their scripts. Thus, even for the artist choosing this theme for a dance drama, Potana's compositions become either an important source or a composition against which he can measure his own.

In Pothana's composition the story begins with Hiranyakasipu's Tapassu (penance). Hence, the Gods go and request Lord Vishnu for protection from Hiranyakasipu's atrocities. Then, the narration goes on to the birth and childhood of Prahlāda. Then Hiranyakasipu hands over Prahlāda to Chanda and Amarka, the two sons of Sukracharya and the remaining episodes are almost in the same order as in Yakshagānams. The Kūchipūdi text, rather than the Mélattūr text, seems to run on the lines of Pothana's composition.

PRAHLĀDA CHARITRA YAKSHAGĀNAM LITERATURE AND SCRIPTS OF THE MÉLATTŪR AND KŪCHIPŪDI PRAHLĀDA CHARITRA PERFORMANCES

From the earliest of the literature in Telugu Prahlāda Charitram has been one of the most recurrent themes.

Yakshagānam literature in Telugu seems to have begun with the Soubhari Charitram of Proluganti Chinna Souri. He called his work as Jakkulakatha which is the other name of the Yakshagānam. But this book is not available today[8]. The next available Yakshagānam is Sugrīva Vijayam of Kandukuri Rudrakavi, but, according to some, there is an opinion that Vipranārāyana Charitra of Chakrapuri Nārāyana is chronologically earlier to Sugrīvavijayam of Kandukuri Rudrakavi[9]. Both these works belong to the 16th century. Next in chronological order is the Vishnu Māyā vilāsam of Kankanti Paparaju which can be dated to around 1600 A.D. Jānakī Parinayam of Tekumalla Rangasayi also belongs to the same period. The first woman composer of Telugu Yakshagānam is Bala Papamba, who composed Akkamahādévi Charitra, which can be dated to the second half of the 16th century. There are several others who composed Yakshagānams during the 16th century.[10]

During the reign of the Nayaka Kings in South (Tanjore, Madurai, etc.) the Yakshagānam literature flourished and reached its peak. During the 17th and 18th centuries, the southern Kingdoms of Tanjore, Madurai, Chenji, Pudukkotai and Mysore became the main centres of Telugu literary activity. During this period Yakshagānam became the dominant form of literature[11]. The large number of Yakshagānams composed during this period could not have been possible without the extensive prevalence of Yakshagānam performances. Who performed these Yakshagānams, whether they belonged to Bhāgavata Mélam like Kūchipūdi or Mélattūr Mélam or whether there were other performing troupes, is not clear. But, interestingly, Raghunatha Nayaka, son of Achyutappa Nayaka, the donor of Mélattūr Agrahāram (Brahmin village) to the Mélattūr performers seems to be the first known composer of Prahlāda Charitra Yakshagānam in the chronological order[12]. Prahlāda Charitra is mentioned among his works, but is not available today. Next author of Prahlāda Charitra in chronological order is Vijayaraghava Nayaka, the King of Tanjore and the son of Raghunatha Nayaka and his work is dated to 1652 A.D. This work is one of the five works of the Vijayaraghava Nayaka available today. S.V. Joga Rao in his Ph.D thesis on the Yakshagānam literature in Telugu does a small introductory review of this work[13]. According to him, Katikamvādu (Baton holder) who became a conventional character in Yakshagānams of the later period is introduced for the first time in the Prahlāda Charitram of

Vijayaraghava Nayaka. Interestingly, this Katikamvāni Vālakam (the behaviour of the Baton Holder) episode is found in the Mélattūr version of Prahlāda Charitra Nātakam also. The next point highlighted by Joga Rao is the colloquial language used in the conversations of Prahlāda's gurus and Pāmula jōgi (the snake charmer) character in Vijayaraghava's Prahlāda Charitram. Joga Rao highlights even the instructions to the performers incorporated within the work composed by Vijayaraghava Nayaka. On the basis of these instructions Joga Rao conclusively declares that this script was used for performances during the 17th century. Similarities between the Mélattūr Prahlāda Charitra Nātakam script and the work of Vijayaraghava Nayaka may be either due to the influence of the Mélattūr performance of Prahlāda Charitra Nātakam on Vijayaraghava Nayaka or vice versa. The next important composer of the Prahlāda Charitra Nātakam is Mélattūr Venkata Rama Sastry during late 18th Century and early 19th century. Venkata Rama Sastry was member of the Mélattūr Bhāgavata Mélam and is said to have composed 12 Yakshagānams, all in Telugu. The Prahlāda Charitra Nātakam used today seems to be one of these twelve works. The Mélattūr Bhāgavata Méla Nātakam team claims that the script used by them in contemporary performances of Prahlāda Charitra Nātakam is, in fact, the same as composed by Mélattūr Venkata Rama Sastry.

Tyagaraja seems to have composed Prahlāda Bhakti Vijayam during the same period. But this work does not include several important characters of the Prahlāda Charitra. Prahlāda seems to be the single character of the composition. This seems to be a music centred work in which devotional lyric meant to be sung by the Prahlāda character, is the most dominant portion of the script.

Prahlāda Nātakam became recurrent more during the 19th and early 20th centuries. Tadipatri Laxmana Dasa who composed Prahlāda Nātakam during the second half of the 19th century mentions Prahlāda Nātakam of Vedachala Tirunarayanacharyulu and Yadavadasu as works earlier to his[14]. Prahlāda Charitra Nātakam of some other authors is also mentioned in Joga Rao's book. For example, there is a book by Bodicharla Subba Kavi of

Kurnool district. He seems to have composed this work in later 19th century. According to Joga Rao, in this work the name of Hiranyakasipu's wife is Susila instead of Lilavati[15]. Katikamvādu (Baton holder) character speaks in Hindi, Tamil and Kannada languages in this work[16]. One Nischinta Yakambarayya also seems to have composed a Prahlāda Vijayam[17].

The work of Vedahchala Tirunarayanacharyulu mentioned here appears to be very important since the Kūchipūdi Prahlāda Nātakam script seems to be mainly based on this work. Vedantam Parvatisam, who is the compiler of the Kūchipūdi Prahlāda Nātakam (Yakshagānam) available in print today, mentions Vedachala Tirunarayanacharyulu and Tiruvallikkeni Ramanujacharyulu as the authors of the scripts on which his compilation is based. In the preface of this printed book he even mentions[18],

> "It seems Sri Vedachala Tirunarayanacharyulu and Sri Tiruvellekkeni Ramanujacharyulu seems to have handed over the manuscripts of the Prahlāda Nātakam composed by them to my ancestors 150 years ago".

He mentions two other names Sri Perumbuduruvaru and Bokkaramabrahmam as the composers of the lyrics incorporated in his compositions[19]. A lot of Hindi/ Urdu Language and Hindustani music are incorporated in this script of Tirunarayanacharyulu along with the Telugu language and Carnatic music (Joga Rao mentions the family name of the Tirunarayanacharuyulu as Vedala whereas Vedantam Parvatisam mentions it as Vedachala. Joga Rao mentions that the work is dedicated to Sesha Saila Dhamudu, Lord Venkateswara and Vedantam Parvatisam mentions the makutam (dedicative addressing) of Uragasailavasa (probably Lord Venkateswara only)[20]. Vedantam Rattayya Sarma gives more particulars about this handing over of the Prahlāda Charitra scripts to the Kūchipūdi team by Vedachala Tirunarayanacharyulu and Tiruvallekkeni Ramanujacharyulu. According to him, around 1875[21] the Kūchipūdi team happened to have camped in Nellore, performing several kalapās like Bhāmākalāpam, Golla Kalāpam and Dādinamma. Vedachala Tirunarayanacharyulu was among the audiences during these performances. He was immensely impressed by the talent of the Kūchipūdi dancers. He congratulated and admired the team members and during the course of his discussion with the Kūchipūdi team he informed them of the Prahlāda Charitra Nātakam composed by him and asked the team to adopt it to their performance. The team was pleased with the gesture of the great scholar and readily agreed to perform Prahlāda Charitram using the script provided by him. When the team hesitated a little with regard to the finances Vedachala Tirunarayanacharylu volunteered to arrange funds for the performance. The team was doubly happy and performed the Prahlāda Charitram. That was the first ever performance of Prahlāda Charitram by the Kūchipūdi team. During this performance Tiruvellekkeni Ramanujacharyulu was in the audience. He was immensely pleased by the performance and offered the script of Prahlāda Charitra Nātakam composed by him to be made use of by the Kūchipūdi team. The team happily adopted portions of this script into their next performance. From the names of Vedachala Tirunarayanacharyulu and Tiruvallekkeni Ramanujacharyulu it may easily be understood that these authors are Srivaishnavaites. Srivaishnavism is the religious tradition founded by Sriramanujacharya in 12th century. The philosophy of this tradition is known as Vishishtadwita Vedanta. This is a Vishnu centred tradition and as such Bhagavata and the stroy from Bhagavata which are Vishnu centred are of a great significance to Srivaishnavism. It can easily be guessed that the two authors mentioned above had an intense religious intension in composing the scripts (and in handing them over to the Kūchipūdi family) and it can be expected that the script also reflected the religiosity of the authors. Hari Madhavayya[22] contributed to the music composition and choreography in adopting the scripts. According to Vedantam Rattayya Sarma, Hari Madhavayya, in fact, handed over the responsibility of composing a fullfledged Prahlāda Charitra script to his nephew (sister's son) Chinta Venkataramayya, alias Venkata Raidu, popularly known as Balintaramayya[23]. Venkataramayya was a wonderful musician and excellent choreographer and erudite literateuer[24]. According to Rattayya Sarma, today's Prahlāda Charitra performance is basically a legacy of this composition edited by Chinta Venkataramayya. This edition of the performance was taken from place to place by different Kūchipūdi teams who spread out from Kūchipūdi to other places. When Rattayẏa Sarma's team went to perform at different places, they were told that Kūchipūdi performance of Prahlāda Charitram was already well known to them as the performance took place in that area decades ago. Some from the older generation of audiences even guided them in stage settings, etc., by recollecting how the Kūchipūdi team, which performed Prahlāda Charitram there decades ago, did it[25]. According to Rattayya Sarma, the Kūchipūdi team made extensive use of Potana's Prahlāda Charitram verses discussed earlier[26] and they adopted the following verses of Potana's Bhāgavatam[27]:

Mandāra makaranda mādhuryamuna délu

Madhupambu vovune madanamulaku....

Can a honey-bee that floats on (lives on) the nectar of the hibiscus flowers go to (honey less) wild flowers?

Padyam No. 150

According to Rattayya Sarma, the Kūchipūdi team made great use of vachanams (prose dialogues) from Sri Dharmavaram Rama Krishnamacharyulu's Prahlāda Charitram, a mythological (verse, prose, non-dance) drama[28].

Based on the above information we may arrive at the following conclusion about the scripts of Mélattūr and Kūchipūdi Prahlāda Charitra Yakshagānams:

1. Both Mélattūr and Kūchipūdi scripts of Prahlāda Charitra Yakshagānam are products of a long tradition of Prahlāda Charitra Yakshagānam, which is at least 400 years old. The earliest known composition being the one composed by Raghunadha Nayaka towards the end of 16th Century.
2. The Mélattūr script, though found to have influences of the Yakshagānams of Vijaya Raghava Nayaka (17th Century), seems to have been based on the script by Mélattūr Venkatarama Sastry (1743-1809 A.D.).[29]

3. The Kūchipūdi script is based on the scripts of Vedachala Tirunarayanacharyulu and Tiruvellekkeni Ramanaujacharyulu, on one hand, and verses from Potana's Bhāgavatam and prose dialogues from the mythological drama by Dharmavaram Rama Krishnamacharyulu, on the other.

The information that the Kūchipūdi script was first procured from Nellore and the oral history of the Mélattūr performers that they migrated from Pisuvati village[30] in the then Nellore Mandala put together gives us scope to concur that Nellore and its surroundings probably had a vibrant tradition of Prahlāda Charitra Yakhagānams. The Mélattūr team while migrating from the Nellore area took this tradition along with it. The tradition which remained in Nellore got revived through the Kūchipūdi team's interaction with the scholars of Nellore. Probably Mélattūr team's attachment for Prahlāda Charitra Yakshagānam could be explained on the basis of nostalgia because that the Prahlāda Charitra tradition is an ancestral legacy of the Mélattūr artistes.

CONCLUSIONS

The roots of attraction between Prahlāda Charitram in Kūchipūdi and Mélattūr traditions are more than one. The most superficial is that both the traditions are Bhāgavata traditions, i.e., devotional traditions, and, hence, it is quite natural for these two traditions to take up devotional themes like the Prahlāda Charitra, which is in fact a story of victory of devotion. But neither the Kūchipūdi team members nor the Mélattūr Bhāgavatārs give such a reason to justify the significance of the theme. According to the Kūchipūdi Bhāgavatārs, they just like this theme as it is. It is good to perform and gives great scope to exhibit their artistic excellence. Popularity, according to them, is another consideration. Prahlāda Charitra is one of the dance-dramas, which earned them enormous popularity, which they enjoy even today. For the Mélattūr team Prahlāda Charitra has more religious and ritualistic significance. They have to perform Prahlāda Charitra as part of their family vow and worship for Lord Narasimha, the principal deity of the Narasimha temple of Mēlattūr. That is the reason why Mélattūr performers who no longer live on dance, who in fact are well settled in professions other than dance, come back to Mélattūr (some of them all the way from far off countries like U.A.E), just to participate in the performance of Prahlāda Charitra on the Narasimha Jayanthi in the premises of Varadaraja Perumal Temple of Mēlattūr. Both Kūchipūdi and Mélattūr traditions of Prahlāda Charitra performance are related to a long tradition of Narasimha Cult prevalent in Andhra Pradesh. Kūchipūdi tradition is also related to the literary tradition of Narasimha literature in Telugu. For the Mélattūr people, if the theory of migration from the Nellore area is historically valid, Prahlāda Charitra may even have a family significance as an ancestral memoir of their original place of living. The Kūchipūdi performers, who took the original scripts of Prahlāda Charitra from Nellore and from Srivaishnavite scholars, detached it from both the region of Nellore and religiosity of Srivaishnavism and made it one of the themes of their repertoire, giving it the identity and stamp of the Kūchipūdi style of performance. The religiosity and regional strangeness found in the Mélattūr performance might be the continuation of the original Prahlāda Charitra performance. Even the Mélattūr religiosity, as in the case of Kūchipūdi, has nothing to do with Srivaishnavite tradition.

REFERENCES

1. Srimadandhra Mahabhagavatam by Potana, Andhra Pradesh sahitya Academy Publications, Hyderabad, 1983, pp. 4-61.
2. Ibid., pp. 4-61.
3. Interview with Vedantam Rattayya Sarma, dated 3rd December, 1996.
4. Interview with Vedantam Rattayya Sarma, dated 3rd December, 1996.
5. See Iconography, p. 336.
6. See Narasimhacharya, Madabhushini, p. 436.
7. See Narasimhacharya, Madabhushini, p. 32.

8. Andhra Yashagāna Vāngmaya Charitra by S.V. Joga Rao, Andhra University Publications, Waltair 1961, second part, p. 1.

9. Ibid, second part, pp. 9-10.

10. Ibid, second part, pp. 17-22.

11. Telugu Sahitya Samiksa by G. Nagayya, own publication. Tirupati.

12. Andhra Yakshagāna Vāngmaya Charitra by S.V. Joga Rao, Andhra University Publication, Waltair 1961, pp. no. 251-252.

13. Ibid., pp. 261-262.

14. Ibid., p. 369.

15. Ibid., p. 136.

16. Ibid., p. 136.

17. Ibid., p. 200.

18. Kūchipūdi Prahlāda Nātakam (Yakshagānam), compiled by Vedantam Parvatisam, own publication 1981, p. 3.

19. Ibid., p. 3.

20. Ibid, page no. 3 and Andhra Yakshagāna Vāngmaya Charitra by S.V. Joga Rao, Andhra University Publication, 1961, p. 140.

21. Interview with Rattayya Sarma, dated 3rd December 1996.

22. The exact date of Hari Madhavayya is not clearly estabished. In 'who is who' of Kūchipūdi Dance by Jonnalagadda Anuradha, the date of Hari Madhavayya is mentioned as "late 18th and mid 19th centuries".

23. The date of Late Shri Cinta Venkataramayya is mentioned as 1860-1947 by Laksmi Narasimha Sastry Chintalapati, Kūchipūdi Bhāgavatulu, own publication, Tenali, 1983, p. 260.

24. Interview with Rattayya Sarma, 3rd December, 1996.

25. Interview with Rattayya Sarma, 3rd December, 1996.

26. Interview with Rattayya Sarma, 3rd December, 1996.

27. Potana is a 15th century Telugu poet who rendered the Bhagavata purana of Vyasa into Telugu. The book is in metrical verse. The poem under reference is also a verse composed in a meter called sisam. From a dance-theatrical point of view the point to be noted above the inclusion of verses into dance-theatre requires a different style of musical rendering than the usual Yakshagāna style of rendering.

28. Interview with Rattayya Sarma, 3rd December, 1996.

29. Andhra Yakshagana Vāngmaya Charitra by S.V. Joga Rao, Andhra University Publications, 1961, pp. 335-336.

30. Interview with S. Natarajan dated 22nd May, 1995.

3

The Two Prahlāda Yakshagānams: A Macro Level Comparison

Culture and surrounding environment plays an important role in influencing the art forms, including dance, music and theatre. In view of this, it will be interesting to compare Kūchipūdi and Mélattūr performances of Prahlāda Charitra Nātakam, against their cultural backgrounds.

ETHNOGRAPHIC BACKGROUND

Both the Kūchipūdi and Mélattūr villages are Agraharams. An Agraharam is a village where only Brahmins live. The architecture of the houses and the topography of the village are conducive to the traditional Brahminical way of life. The earliest historical document, the famous Machupalli kaifiat, makes a mention of the Kūchipūdi tradition. It also mentions the performers as hailing from the Kūchipūdi village[1]. There is no earlier record to support that this village was a donation to the Kūchipūdi performers as a reward for their performance. However, records of later times established the fact that lands in and around this village were donated to the members of the Kūchipūdi community by Tanisha, one of the Golkonda Kings.[2] The Mélattūr village, according to all the oral histories available, was a donation to Mélattūr artists by Atchyutappa Nayaka, the Tanjore King (1560-1600 A.D.).

Machupalli Kaifiat describes Kūchipūdi tradition as a team, which used to travel from place to place to perform[3]. In contrast, the Mélattūr artists, according to all the oral histories, are depicted as a team which never travelled out of Mélattūr. They never took their performance as a living. Especially, today's Mélattūr team members are all well off and do not depend on their performance for their living. They perform with an attitude of sacrality and reverence, sentiment and vow towards the traditional artistic activity of their lineage. The Kūchipūdi team in all the oral histories is depicted as the one which took its dance performance as a profession and as a living.

The Prahlāda Charitra Nātakam is never performed outside Mélattūr. They perform it only in the Varadaraja Perumal temple premises in Mélattūr (Plate-XI).[4] They do not violate this principle about the place of performance of Prahlāda Charitra Nātakam. The Kūchipūdi team adheres to no such rule and performs the Prahlāda Charitra Nātakam at several places outside Kūchipūdi.

ATTITUDE TOWARDS PRAHLĀDA NĀTAKAM

For the Kūchipūdi team performance of Prahlāda Charitra Nātakam is one of their many performing activities. According to Rattayya Sarma, Kūchipūdi team does not engage itself in any special rehearsal for the performance of Prahlāda Charitra Nātakam. The script of Prahlāda Charitra Nātakam becomes a part of the memory of a huge repertoire of texts for all the team members. Each member grows up hearing and learning the script. There are no specific jobs assigned to specific members of the team. Each member, right from the childhood, learns to execute all the different aspects of the performance right from holding the screen and torches, background and chorus singing, to stage setting and playing of various characters of a given dance drama within the repertoire of the Kūchipūdi tradition. In accordance with their all round abilities, any member of the Kūchipūdi team can execute any role within the Prahlāda Charitra Nātakam. Rattayya Sarma argues that this arrangement prevents last minute upsets due to the non availability of a particular team member[5]. Thus, the Kūchipūdi team does not require notice much in advance for the performance. They are often ready to perform even on the very day of the invitation. In contrast, the Mélattūr team makes advance preparations for Prahlāda Charitra Nātakam performance. Since the performance is not part of their daily routine or vocation, the members feel the need for preparation at least two weeks before the performance of any of their dance dramas. This holds good even for Prahlāda Charitra Nātakam performance. The Mélattūr team members from Bangalore, Madras, Kumbhakonam, U.A.E. and Mélattūr gather at Mélattūr at least two weeks in advance to the day of Prahlāda Charitra Nātakam performance. They rehearse regularly during these days and, thus, gear themselves up for the great event of the year, viz., Prahlāda Charitra Nātakam in the premises of the Varadaraja Perumal Temple of Mēlattūr. Each member of the Mélattūr team is assigned a particular job in the performance.

Mélattūr team members observe strict rules of purity and pollution during the performance days. Each member observes "madi" (purity maintained through wearing specially washed clothes and a special head bath and with restrictions of not touching any 'impure' person or material). The Narasimha role player fasts for the entire day of the performance to maintain purity and devotion. The Kūchipūdi team members recollect that even the Kūchipūdi performers of earlier generation used to maintain similar restrictions[6], especially in connection with Prahlāda Charitra Nātakam performance. Today, the Kūchipūdi team members are not found to be so particular about these restrictions. Oral histories reveal that Kūchipūdi practitioners began giving up these restrictions several generations ago for all performances other than Prahlāda Charitra Nātakam. But with regard to Prahlāda Charitra Nātakam austerities were maintained till recently. The non austere approach of the Kūchipūdi team is now spreading to Prahlāda Charitra Nātakam also.

The Mélattūr team takes the selection of characters seriously. The major characters of Prahlāda Charitra Nātakam are assigned to specific members of the team. Performers from the same community are invited from different places, like Chennai, Bangalore to enact all other minor characters.

Each performer plays a specific character with great involvement and takes his performance seriously and gets identified with the same. Playing any character of the dance drama is a part of the worship of Lord Narasimha. Natarajan, the present organiser of one of the Mélattūr teams, feels that Lord Narasimha himself oversees the casting from time to time.[7] According to him, when a particular performer ages, Lord Narasimha appears in the organizer's dream and asks him to hand over that particular character to a specific younger member of the team. As an example, Natarajan quotes the incident of how the character of Hiranyakasipu was given to Kumar (Plate-XII) when Swaminadhan playing that character aged. Lord Narasimha appeared in Natarajan's dream and asked Swaminadhan to stop playing the character of Hiranyakasipu as he was too old to perform and, therefore, hand it over to the younger member Kumar. Swaminadhan did not accept the decision in the beginning, as he was too attached to his performance and was not ready to give it up. But after coming to know that it was Lord Narasimha's order he yielded and Kumar became the Hiranyakasipu (Plate-XIII) from the next performance onwards. When Swaminadhan saw Kumar in the Costume of Hiranyakasipu he shouted in admiration and went on applauding the performance with loud shouts of excitement throughout the performance. He felt secure about his legacy being taken forward by an able Kumar[8]. This response by G. Swaminadhan clearly reveals that his earlier resistance to give up performance was out of attachment for the art form than out of egoistic consideration. His readiness to appreciate the younger talent reflects his noble personality as an artist. Natarajan who played the Līlāvati character for almost 35 years would give it up on the instructions of Lord Narasimha and would hand it over to Prasanna, who has been performing minor woman roles.

In the Kūchipūdi team the major responsibility is that of the negotiation with the sponsors of the programme and distribution of the money among the members of the team. According to Rattayya Sarma this is not an easy task. Apart from artistic satisfaction the main incentive for the performers is the remuneration, which is their livelihood. This usually leads to psychological problems, and to manage them the organizer needs great organizational skills. In the Mélattūr team the organizer has a great responsibility with regard to finances because the Mélattūr Prahlāda Charitra Nātakam performance must take place irrespective of the availability of a sponsorship. Usually, sponsorship is meagre. In fact, according to Kumar of Bangalore, a team member, who plays the role of Hiranyakasipu of Natarajan's group, one of the major reasons for Natarajan going to U.A.E. is to earn enough finances through his own job to sustain the tradition of the annual performance of Prahlāda Charitra Nātakam[9]. Natarajan has assumed the responsibility of taking care of the financial requirements of the performance, including the arrangements for stay of several guests at Mélattūr during the performance. This indicates the extraordinary commitment and devotion of the Mélattūr community for their art form.

Plate-XI Premises of the Varadaraja Perumal Temple, the Venue of Mélattūr Prahlāda Charitra Nātakam Performance.

Plate–XII Kumar as Hiranyakasipu in the Mélattūr Prahlāda Nātakam Performance.

MAKEUP AND COSTUME

The Kūchipūdi team prepares its own make up material and the team members with their professional skills are adept at makeup. Rattayya Sarma reminisces that the traditional Kūchipūdi performers used to prepare props like the Gada (mace), etc., using the sticks and other raw material available in the village where the team was performing. Their travel kit used to include the makeup material also[10]. This material included the traditional powders, wigs, etc. But the teams have, now-a-day, switched over to engaging a makeup man and adapting to modern makeup techniques. Contrarily, the Mélattūr team never treated makeup as a part of its professional activity. It always depended on the help of a makeup man performing similar duties in the traditional Tamil Folk Theatre. But the Mélattūr costumes have its own identity (they adopt the attire of Krishnadevaraya) and the makeup man always keeps it under consideration and adapts his makeup technique to the traditional costume of the Mélattūr team.

VENUE AND STAGE

Venue of performance and stage arrangements is another aspect in which Kūchipūdi and Mélattūr Prahlāda Charitra Nātakams differ greatly. The traditional Kūchipūdi Prahlāda Charitra Nātakam performance was just like any other traditional Yakshagānam performance, an open air street performance. Any street corner can turn into the venue for the Kūchipūdi Prahlāda Charitra Nātakam performance. Traditionally, there was no separate elevation for the stage. The audience and performers used to be on the same level on the ground. A portion of the ground used to be cleaned and levelled for the performance. A circular white powder drawing was drawn around the stage so as to keep away the evil spirits.

Rangapuja (stage ritual) is performed to ward off evil spirits. The makeshift screen is brought on to the stage and the characters enter from behind the screen. After the entry the screen itself exits. Rattayya Sarma says that Prahlāda Charitra Nātakam requires some special stage arrangements like creating a pillar from which Narasimha has to crash out. He recollects that in the early days of his performance some from the audience themselves helped in making such arrangements, recollecting from their own memory of having watched Prahlāda Charitra Nātakam performance by the ancestors of the present Kūchipūdi teams[11]. The traditional stage setting has gradually evolved into an elevated circular stage made up of tables which were part of the traditional furnished houses. Now-a-day, the performances are being staged in the modern auditoriums. The Mélattūr Prahlāda Charitra Nātakam performance takes place only in the premises of the Varadaraja Perumal Temple of Mēlattūr. In the street (teru) and in front of the temple (Plate-XIV) a pandal (a covered structure erected for performance) is raised (Plate-XV) in the direction facing the main entrance of the Varadaraja Perumal temple. This pandal is erected in front of the temple within the clusters of houses.

Spectators squat in the space available in the pandal. Some lean back on to the walls of the veranda in front of the houses close to the pandal. Some bring their own benches and settle down in some convenient place. Some of the guests are provided with a few chairs (Plate-XVI) in the front part of the pandal. The significant aspect is that the performers face the main entrance of the temple during their performance, symbolising obeisance to the deity of the temple (Figure-II). At the end of the performance, the Narasimha character is worshipped in the same way as the deity in the temple (Plate-XVII). After the worship they offer Pānakam (Plate-XVIII) (sweet water drink made up of Jaggery), the favourite drink of Lord Narasimha, to the Narasimha character just as it is offered to the deity Narasimha in the temple. This drink is made in five or six huge vessels and is offered to the audience as teertham (sacred water). All these features of the Mélattūr Prahlāda Charitra Nātakam performance clearly establish the devotional and ritual nature of the performance.

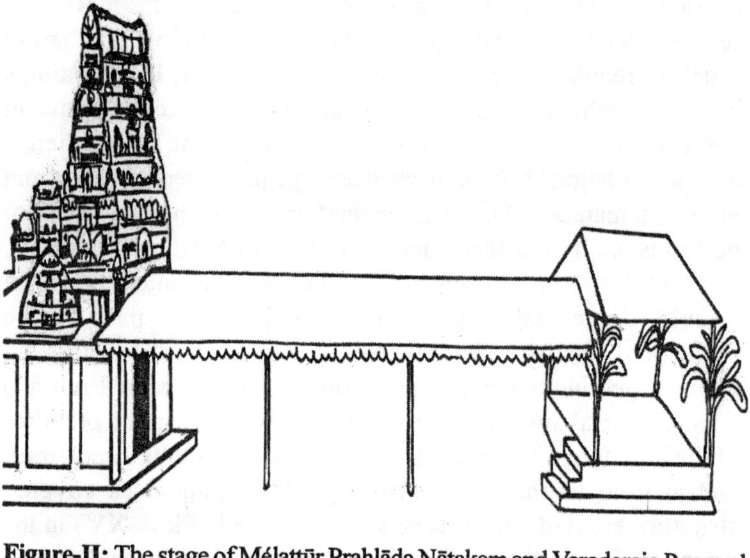

Figure-II: The stage of Mélattūr Prahlāda Nātakam and Varadaraja Perumal temple facing each other with a street joining the two (Drawing by Lakshmana Murthy).

The common feature of the Kūchipūdi and Mélattūr Prahlāda Charitra Nātakams is that both of them follow the devotional version of the Prahlāda story, according to which Hiranyakasipu in his previous birth was the doorkeeper of the Lord Vishnu. He was longing to see Lord Vishnu and get killed in his hands. In both the Prahlāda Charitra Nātakams, Hiranyakasipu thanks Prahlāda (Plate-XIX) for having helped him see Lord Vishnu who he could not see earlier despite great efforts. This expression is intended as a pun. At a superficial level this appears to be an expression of the arch enemy of the Lord Vishnu who rejoices at the prospect of destroying the enemy. This also expresses the eagerness of the doorkeeper of the Lord Vishnu (who is born as Hiranyakasipu) to see his Lord. In the Kūchipūdi Prahlāda Charitra Nātakam when Diti laments the deaths of Hiranyaksha, Hiranyakasipu consoles her saying that his brother was lucky to have died in the hands of Lord Vishnu, the liberator of all the souls. But this devotional nature of the story does not translate into a devotional performance in the Kūchipūdi tradition of Prahlāda Charitra Nātakam.

DETAILS OF THE PERFORMANCE SCRIPT AND TECHNIQUE OF STORY PRESENTATION

Based on the above comparison of the backgrounds of the two performing styles of Prahlāda Charitra Nātakam one may infer that the Mélattūr Nātakam is performed in greater detail than the Kūchipūdi Nātakam. But interestingly in opposition to this expectation, traditional Kūchipūdi performance of Prahlāda Charitra Nātakam is more detailed and elaborate than the Mélattūr performance. The traditional Kūchipūdi Prahlāda Charitra Nātakam used to be performed for three full nights. The Mélattūr performance of Prahlāda Charitra Nātakam lasts only for five and half hours a single night.

The traditional Kūchipūdi performance of Prahlāda Charitra Nātakam begins with the episode of Hiranyakasipu's mother, Diti, mourning the death of her son Hiranyaksha and a conversation between Diti and Hiranyakasipu. The next episode includes Hiranyakasipu's *tapas* (penance) to please Lord Brahma and a lyric of Līlāvati trying to stop Hiranyakasipu and expressing her

Plate-XIII: S. Kumar of the Mélattūr team is the present Hiranyakasipu of Mélattūr Prahlāda Nātakam.

Plate-XIV: The Street, in front of the temple, with thatched and tiled houses on either side emanating from the main entrance of the temple. Note: the Pandal erected for Mélattūr festival.

Plate-XV: Street in front of the temple with thatched and tiled houses on either sides leading towards the stage erected for the Melattur festival.

Plate-XVI: Some of the guests of Mélattūr Prahlāda Nātakam are provided with a few chairs in the front part of the pandal.

Plate-XVII Worship of Narasimha dancer as part of Mélattūr Prahlāda Nātakam, Natarajan, reciting hymns as Bhoomi Devi and Prahlāda performers watch on.

Plate-XVIII: Offering of the sweet Jaggery water to Narasimha dancer by Bhāgavatārs and other members of the Bhāgavata Méla watch on.

inability to bear separation from her husband. Hiranyakasipu does not yield to her request. He instructs his ministers to look after his kingdom well in his absence. The next episode includes a lyric of eulogy performed by Hiranyakasipu in praise of Lord Brahma. Further to this there is a conversation between Devendra and Brihaspati followed by the kidnapping of Līlāvati by Devendra and a conversation between Līlāvati and Devendra. Narada (the divine sage, the greatest devotee of Lord Narayana who keeps traversing all over the world) enters and persuades Devendra to allow Līlāvati to go along with him. In the next episode, the scene shifts to Hiranyakasipu's *tapas* where Brahma appears and sanctions him the boon.

The next episode involves a lyric describing the glory of Hiranyakasipu's return to his Kingdom. At this juncture, Narada enters and informs Hiranyakasipu of Devendra's deed of kidnapping Līlāvati and how he (Narada) protected her. Hiranyakasipu gets angry with Devendra and orders the Rakshasas (demons) to create havoc for Devas (gods) and their king (Devendra) and take them into custody. The demons execute the order when the door keeper informs Hiranyakasipu of the entry of midwife and she informs Hiranyakasipu about the birth of his son. Hiranyakasipu celebrates this news and orders for the release of the imprisoned Devas (Gods). Sukracharya, the guru of the demons enters at this juncture and a conversation between Sukracharya and Hiranyakasipu ensues about the new born prince and the name 'Prahlāda 'for the baby is decided. Hiranyakasipu then sends his son with Chanda and Amarka, the traditional teachers of the demon community.

In the Mélattūr performance the story involving the above episodes is cut short. The Mélattūr performance begins with the entry of Sukracharya who informs Hiranyakasipu about the death of Hiranyaksha. Hiranyakasipu gets into a rage and resolves to avenge his brother's death. Līlāvati tries to pacify him. At this juncture, Hiranyakasipu reminisces about his *tapas* and the ensuing boon from Lord Brahma and the resultant immunity to death. Hiranyakasipu orders his demons to go in search of Lord Vishnu and locate him. The demons return back and inform their failure in locating Lord Vishnu. Prahlāda enters at this juncture and enquires from his father the reason for his enmity with Lord Vishnu. Chanda and Amarka enter the scene and Hiranyakasipu hands over his son to them and ask them to teach the boy enmity with Lord Vishnu. This episode of Chanda and Amarka teaching Prahlāda the demonical tenets, Prahlāda not receptive to the same, etc., is common between the Kūchipūdi and Mélattūr Prahlāda Charitra Nātakams. But in the Mélattūr performance this episode is stretched longer than in the Kūchipūdi performance. The episode is spread over nearly seven scenes in Mélattūr performance whereas in the Kūchipūdi Prahlāda Charitra Nātakam this is done in two scenes.

In the Mélattūr form Prahlāda tells his mates in the Gurukula (traditional school) that he acquired devotion for Narayana (Vishnu) from Narada who initiated him into Vishnu devotion while he was in his mother's womb. Though in the printed version of the Kūchipūdi script of Prahlāda Charitra Nātakam this version of Prahlāda revealing the reason for his devotion to Vishnu to his school mates is found, but is not presented in the actual performances.

In both Mélattūr and Kūchipūdi Prahlāda Charitra Nātakams, the next episode is Hiranyakasipu's evaluation of his son's learning which angers him. In both the versions, Līlāvati enters the scene. In the Mélattūr version there is a lyric in which Līlāvati begs for pardon for the child. In the Kūchipūdi version this is depicted in a small conversation. In both Kūchipūdi and Mélattūr performances this episode is followed by the episode of a series of punishments meted out to Prahlāda like subjecting him to snake bites, making him drink poison, getting him trampled by elephants, throwing him down from high mountains, etc. This is depicted through several scenes. Certain incidents like trampling of Prahlāda by elephants, etc., are only narrated. In the Kūchipūdi performance it is said that a masked elephant character appeared on the stage in the scene[12]. In fact, there is a daruvu (lyric), viz., 'Vedale nadigo mada gajamu' (lo thus starts off the stout elephant) in the Kūchipūdi Prahlāda Charitra Nātakam's printed script and also in the oral tradition. This is not seen in the Mélattūr performance. But in both Kūchipūdi and Mélattūr Prahlāda Charitra Nātakams there are entries of snake charmer, poisoner, wrestlers, etc.

After this episode, Prahlāda is sent back to the Gurukula for another attempt to reforming him in the Kūchipūdi Prahlāda Charitra Nātakam. There are scenes of this second attempt at teaching Prahlāda. In the Kūchipūdi version the boy comes back and an argument ensues between Hiranyakasipu and Prahlāda. In the Mélattūr Prahlāda Charitra Nātakam the episode of the second attempt at teaching Prahlāda is not found. The performance directly proceeds from the episode of punishment to the episode of arguments between Hiranyakasipu and Prahlāda. In the Kūchipūdi Prahlāda Charitra Nātakam, Chanda and Amarka, on the orders of Hiranyakasipu, create through witchcraft an evil spirit called 'Kritti' which attempts to devour Prahlāda. Kritti is unable to reach Prahlāda, who is immersed in Haribhajan (singing the praise of Lord Vishnu) and boomerangs on Chanda and Amarka. The demon teachers seek shelter of Prahlāda. As Prahlāda utters the

Narayana mantra evil spirit gets killed. Chanda and Amarka narrate this incident to Hiranyakasipu who gets extremely infuriated and asks his son to show Lord Vishnu in a pillar opposite to him. In the Mélattūr Prahlāda Charitra Nātakam the episode of Kritti is not found. The argument between Hiranyakasipu and Prahlāda directly leads to Hiranyakasipu asking Prahlāda to show Lord Vishnu in the pillar opposite him. Hereafter, in the episode of Narasimha breaking out of the pillar the Kūchipūdi team also adopts flash back technique and narrative intermissions. The Mélattūr performance could also be a briefer version of a longer performance tradition in the past (as they also use the flash back technique and narrative intermissions). But the Mélattūr team members claim that their present day version of the performance is exactly the same as the oldest and the earliest of their performances and strictly follows the script composed by Mélattūr Venkatarama Sastry. But unless the original script of Mélattūr Venkatarama Sastry becomes available this cannot be confirmed[13].

PERFORMANCE PROGRAMMING

In the Mélattūr Prahlāda Charitra Nātakam performance the entire story of Prahlāda Charitra Nātakam is narrated in brief as a part of the pre story of the performance. Killing of Hiranyakasipu, Prahlāda singing the praise of Lord Narasimha, Prahlāda and others trying to pacify Lord Narasimha, the pacified Lord Narasimha blessing Prahlāda are all common between Kūchipūdi and Mélattūr Prahlāda Charitra Nātakams.

From the above comparison it is evident that the Kūchipūdi version of the Prahlāda Charitra story has more details than the Mélattūr one. In fact, the Kūchipūdi story adheres to the purāna version. In the Mélattūr Prahlāda Charitra Nātakam the brevity becomes possible through the narration of the entire story in the beginning of the performance itself and through the flash back technique adapted at different junctures.

Kūchipūdi version of Prahlāda Charitra Nātakam performance, described earlier, is based on the printed and oral versions and from the memories of Kūchipūdi performers. Today's

Kūchipūdi Prahlāda Charitra Nātakam is not as long as this. Now-a-day, the Kūchipūdi performance concludes within a single night and sometimes within one or two hours in the briefer versions.

The pre-story part of the performance of the Kūchipūdi and Mélattūr Prahlāda Charitra Nātakams has a few similarities. The Kūchipūdi programme begins with Pūrvarangam (pre-stage), which includes *(i)* Nandi Vachanam (opening narration), *(ii)* Vinayaka Stuti (praise) and *(iii)* Amba Stuti. The Mélattūr Prahlāda Charitra Nātakam begins with Todaimangalam, which includes Vinayaka Stuti and Anjaneya Stuti. In the Mélattūr version this part is followed by a unique humorous intervention by a comic, slim and tall character called 'Konangi' (Plate-XX). Konangi is a fictitious, idiomatic metaphor for a mischievous character popular in the coastal areas of Andhra Pradesh. Konté Konangi (mischievous Konangi) is the usual expression used in reference to him. This character enters the stage, performs a comic dance and exits. According to the Mélattūr team, there is a myth associated with 'Konangi'. Once Vinayaka swallowed the chakra of Lord Vishnu and the Gods tried their best to get the weapon out of Vinayaka's belly. Failing in their attempts, they created Konangi who through his mischievous humour made Vinayaka burst out into a loud laughter which made the disc weapon to come out of his belly. In the Mélattūr version the Konangi's dance is followed by the entry of two Bhāgavatārs (Plate-XXI) who sing the lyrics of Prahlāda Pattābhisékam Sabdam composed by Mélattūr Venkatarama Sastry. Now-a-day, the Mélattūr team performs dance to this lyric. This is followed by the singing of the Vinayaka Pravesam (entry) lyric, discussed in the earlier chapter. Then the Bhāgavatār anchor narrates the story in prose from the left side (for the audience) of the stage in brief in a Yakshagāna type of recital. A dancer donning the Vinayaka mask then dances to the lyrics "Ganapathi vaché" rendered by the Bhāgavatār. After concluding the song, the Bhāgavatār worships Vinayaka by offering a coconut, etc., in front of the dancer wearing the Vinayaka mask (Plate-XXII).

All these pre-story elements are not found in the Kūchipūdi Prahlāda Charitra Nātakam. It directly proceeds from the Amba Stuti to the entry of 'Vétrahastudu' (the baton holder). This Vẹtrahastudu enters the stage, in the Mélattūr Prahlāda Charitra Nātakam after the Ganapathi Worship. Vétrahastudu is called 'Katikamvādu' in the Mélattūr version (Plate-XXIII). In fact, Katikamvādu is the native Telugu word for the Sanskrit word 'Vétrahastudu'. Even today in the Andhra villages there is a traditional job of a cane holding person called 'Katikamvādu, Katikāyana', etc. The cane in the hands of the Katikamvādu is a symbol of the power of the state. Traditionally, this cane holding person used to lead the king and announce his arrival. Chōpudāru is an Urdu word for Katikamvādu. Interestingly, in the Kūchipūdi script the word Chōpudāru is used along with the usage of different languages such as Urdu, Marathi, etc., to announce the arrival of the King Hiranyakasipu. In the Mélattūr version 'Katikamvādu' speaks only Telugu. Here again, the Mélattūr version has an interesting variation in comparison to the Kūchipūdi Prahlāda Charitra Nātakam. The announcement of the arrival of Hiranyakasipu is followed by the arrival of Hiranyakasipu in both Kūchipūdi and Mélattūr Prahlāda Charitra Nātakams. But in the Mélattūr Prahlāda Charitra Nātakam the arrival (entry of Hiranyakasipu) is followed by the entry of the several other major characters like Līlāvati, Prahlāda and Sukracharya. The entry lyrics for all these characters are sung by the supporting singers. In the Ķūchipūdi Prahlāda Charitra Nātakam the entry of Hiranyakasipu after the announcement of Katikamvādu is followed by a royal court scene where Hiranyakasipu will be discussing the affairs of the state with his ministers. Then enter the secret informers of the King, who announce their victory in the destruction of temples, etc. This is followed by the entry of Diti, mother of Hiranyakasipu who grieves the death of Hiranyaksha, as described earlier in this chapter.

The elaborate pre-story performance in the Mélattūr Prahlāda Charitra Nātakam indicates the orthodoxy of the team in following the traditional rituals. The Kūchipūdi team probably avoids all these details in order to sustain the audience interest.

CONCLUSION OF PERFORMANCE

The reasons for the Kūchipūdi team following the detailed version of the story and the Mélattūr team following the brief version can be explained from a different perspective. The entire Mélattūr performance is marked by a predominant melodrama. Each scene is stretched through long conversations and long lyrics. Each dialogue is executed with a slow and deliberate pronunciation. There is an extreme emphasis on the emotions. Contrastingly, the Kūchipūdi Prahlāda Charitra Nātakam conversations and lyrics are shorter, pronounced and sung faster and the melodrama is conspicuously absent in face of the fast action, drama and humour running through the various incidents of the story.

Plate-XIX: The Hiranyakasipu gleefully thanks Prahlāda for having helped him to see Lord Vishnu.

Plate-XX: Konangi, the slim tall clown character of Mélattūr Prahlāda Nātakam, enters holding the napkin parodying the Dancers hand movements.

Plate-XXI: The Bhāgavatārs dancers in the traditional costumes of Mélattūr Bhāgavata Méla enter after Konangi exits as part of the Todaimangalam.

Plate-XXII: Worship of Vinayaka dancer in the Mélattūr Prahlāda Nātakam. Note: Bhāgavatārs offering coconut.

Another distinction of the Mélattūr performance is the marked Tamil accent found in the pronunciation of the Telugu prose and lyrics. The slow and stretched performance of the Mélattūr team does not consider the aspect of sustaining the audience interest, where as the Kūchipūdi performers proclaim that they essentially perform for their audiences[14]. The Mélattūr team members are equally clear that they perform for themselves[15].

TECHNIQUE OF MUSIC AND DANCE

The prolonging nature of the Mélattūr performance is found in the musical composition also. Each syllable of the lyric is stretched through several beats of singing. Even the rhythm (Tālam) adapted indicates a slow and stretched performance. Choreography and different aspects of abhinaya, including Āngikābhinayam, establish the leisurely presentation in the Mélattūr form. Contrastingly, the music and dance found in the Kūchipūdi Prahlāda Charitra Nātakam is consciously faster, dynamic, versatile and variegated and is attractive to the audience. The dance and music aspects of the performance of Kūchipūdi and Mélattūr Prahlāda Charitra Nātakams will be analysed in greater detail in the next chapter.

REFERENCES

1. "Studies in the history of the thrid dynasty of Vijayanagara" By N. Venkata Ramaiah, Appendix-6C, Pages 462-463. As cited in Kūchipūdi Bhāgavatulu, by Laxminarsimha Sastry Chintalapati, own Publications, Tenali, 1983, p. 28.

2. 1672-1687 A.D., Ibid, pp. 108-116.

3. Ibid., p. 28.

4. Interview with S. Kumar, dated 1st December 1996.

5. Interview with Rattayya Sarma, dated 3rd December 1996.

6. Interview with Rattayya Sarma dated 3rd December 1996.

7. There is a theory that the Kūchipūdi team restricted their performances only to male members on account of the purity - pollution observances only.

8. Interview with S. Natarajan, dated 22nd May, 1996.

9. Interview with S. Kumar 1st December, 1996. He Says, "In fact Mélattūr team includes Prahlāda Charitra Nātakam into a week long dance-drama festival in which other dance dramas of Mélattūr repertoire like Harishcandra, Ushā Parinayam, etc., are also performed. Mr. Natrajan hosts the entire festival and the finances earned by him are handy for the hospitality for a big number of distinguished guests".

10. Interview with Vedantam Rattayya Sarma, dated 3rd December, 1996.

11. Interview with Vedantam Rattayya Sarma, dated 3rd December, 1996.

12. Interview with Vedantam Rattayya Sarma, dated 3rd December, 1996.

13. Even after consistent effort this script could not be procured from the Mélattūr team.

14. Interview with Ramanadham, Rattayya Sarma and Vedantarn Parvatisam, dated 3rd December, 1996.

15. Interview with S. Natarajan and S. Kumar, dated 22nd May, 1996.

4

The Two Prahlāda Yakshagānams: A Micro Level Comparison

The identities of the Mélattūr and Kūchipūdi Prahlāda Charitra Nātakam performances are more intricately reflected in the details of the technique of their performances.

RASA SEQUENCE

Since all Nātya aims at evoking the intended Rasa in the spectator, the various aspects of Nātya technique are centred on rasa composition in the Kūchipūdi and Mélattūr Prahlāda Charitra Nātakam performances reveals that the two performances do not differ much in this aspect. As outlined in the previous chapter the Kūchipūdi performance presents more details of the story than the Mélattūr performance. The first episode of the Kūchipūdi performance, namely Hiranyaksha's death and Hiranyakasipu being reminded of it by his mother, has an intense atmosphere of Karuna (Pathos). Here, it is Diti who is the ālambana vibhāva (rasa holding character) for Karuna (Pathos). Diti sings a verse laden with pathos. In response to this Hiranyakasipu sings a lyric "Yenduké nīvitula" (why [do you do] my dear lady like this) (Rāgam: Āhiri, Tālam: Misrachāpu), which has the bhakti (devotional) element in it. Hiranyakasipu proceeds to perform *tapas* (accompanied by verse and prose). At this, Līlāvati responds with a lyric asking her husband not to leave her to suffer from separation. This is a pathetic lyric "itulabaluka taguna" (is it proper (on your part) to speak like this) (Rāgam: Nilāmbari, Tālam: Tripuṭa).

Next to this, there is a Samvāda Daruvu (conversational lyric) "Vataphaladhāri" (the holder of the banyan fruit) sung in Rāgam Ānandabhairavi, Tālam Ādi by Hiranyakasipu and Līlāvati, which has a mixture of Tapovīra (zeal of penance) of Hiranyakasipu and Karuna (Pathos) of Līlāvati. Hiranyakasipu instructs his ministers to look after the kingdom well (prose) and then the lyric "ninné nammiti...." (I trusted you alone) is sung by Hiranyakasipu in praise of Brahma, which has Bhakti (devotion) as the rasa (Rāgam: Punnāgavarāli, Tālam: Misrachāpu). Then there is a sandhi (narrative verse), which has a powerful bhayanaka (terror) effect, describing Hiranyakasipu's *tapas* (penance) as terrifying for all the worlds especially to Indra. There is a conversation between Indra and Brihaspati, which continues in the same element of fear. In the next episode, Indra kidnaps Līlāvati and she responds beginning with an element of roudra (anger) but immediately changing into Karuna (pathos) with the lyric "taguna suranādha," (Is it proper [on your part] oho Lord of the Gods) sung in Hindustani tōdi, tisrachāpu. Here there is an intervention by Narada through a verse and lyric "viduvunīpaddhati" (change your ways) sung in Rāgam Kāmbhōji, Tisragati, which has the element of the santa (detachment) with a tone of pacification. When the scene shifts to Hiranyakasipu's tapas (penance) Brahma appears and talks to Hiranyakasipu through verses and expresses admiration and showers blessings. Hiranyakasipu's response in the form of verses has a tone of obedience and devotion. After the boons are sanctioned by Brahma Hiranyakasipu responds with the emotion of roudra (anger) and vīra (valorous) mixed together. But this creates a feeling of Bhayanaka (fear). Here, Narada enters and engages in a conversation with the Chōpudār which has hāsya (humour). Probably this conversation is meant to provide relief from the continuous serious emotions like anger, fear and pathos. Narada hands over Līlāvati to Hiranyakasipu (There is a dwipada verse here). Coming to know of Indra kidnapping his wife, Hiranyakasipu gets angry (verse and prose). Hiranyakasipu's actions are full of roudra (anger), which evokes the Bhayanaka (fear) element in the audience. Later, the news of Prahlāda's birth is conveyed to Hiranyakasipu and there is a great mood of celebration all around. Sukracharya's entry is with a pravesa daruvu.

Sukracharya's conversation is full of humour. In the next episode Hiranyakasipu converses with his son through the lyric "rāra kumāra" (common my dear son) (Rāgam: Punnāgavarāli, Tālam: Misrachāpu), which is full of vātsalya (parental affection). Prahlāda's dwipada in response to this has santa (detachment) to which Hiranyakasipu responds in roudra (anger). Hiranyakasipu sends word for Chanda and Amarka, whose conversation is humorous. Hiranyakasipu's farewell to Prahlāda is full of vātsalya (parental affection) "chaduvaboyi..." (Having gone for studies) (Rāgam: Śahana, Tālam: Ādi). The following episode of Prahlāda's learning under Chanda and Amarka is humorous. The episode also has devotional lyrics "viduvajālanayya", "danujādhipa..." (I cannot give up, my dear Lord of the demons) and "vinumu chadivi..." (Listen, having studied) sung by Prahlāda (Rāgam: Punnāgavarāli, Tālam: Ādi, Kāmbhōji, Ādi and Bhairavi, Ādi, respectively). The conversation between Hiranyakasipu and Prahlāda includes Hiranyakasipu's lyric "yevaru bōdhinchinārura..." (Who taught [you] (Rāgam: nādanāmakriya, Tālam: Ādi), which is full of roudra (anger) mixed with vātsalya (parental affection). Another lyric "itula balkeda vémira..." (Why do you speak like this my dear) by Hiranyakasipu in kāpi and Ādi is highly persuasive with a tone of parental affection. Prahlāda replies to this in lyric "tanuvunu benchina..." (Enlarge the body) more in renunciation rather than devotion (Raga: Śahana, Tāla: Ādi). Hiranyakasipu gets angry with the teachers Chanda and Amarka (verse). Here Līlāvati enters and there is a Samvāda daruvu "valadurāyanna..."(don't my dear don't) (Conversational lyric between Līlāvati and Prahlāda) (Rāgam: Mukhāri, Tālam: Misrachāpu), which features Līlāvati's fear, pathos and parental affection and Prahlāda's detachment in the mood of bhakti (devotion). The lyric "teliya jālavémira" (why don't you realize) by Hiranyakasipu when he decrees punishment to Prahlāda (Rāgam: Ārabhi, Tālam: Ādi) is with full of terrifying anger. There is also a Samvāda daruvu "dānavéndra sutuni paina" (on the son of the Lord of the demons) between Līlāvati and Hiranyakasipu (Rāgam: Janjulahi, Hamsadhwani, Tālam: Rupakam). Then begins the trail of punishments meted out to Prahlāda.

The first punishment inflicted by the wrestlers with the lyric "endulakégévura" (where do you go my dear) portrays terrifying vīra (valorous zeal) sentiment (Rāgam: Kédāragoula, Tālam: Misrachāpu). Prahlāda's lyric "jattivālla lāra" (oh muscled men) is devotional in a preaching tone (Rāgam: Śankarābharanam, Tālam: Rupakam). The wrestlers collapse after the devotional lyric of Prahlāda, which leads to an atmosphere of surprise and amazement. There is a repeat of Prahlāda's devotion and Līlāvati's persuasion. The next punishment is almost a repeat of the earlier punishment seene. There is again a conversation between Prahlāda and Hiranyakasipu, a repeat of persuasion, devotion and anger and again persuasion by Līlāvati. The next punishment scene begins with the serpent charmer's entry followed by a long conversation with Singi (female clown) and Bhāgavatār (mediator). After this, there is almost a repeat of the earlier punishment scene, but Prahlāda returns back singing "ninnu nammina vādara" (I have faith in you my Lord) in Rāgam Yaman, Tālam Ādi. Hiranyakasipu again persuades Prahlāda with parental affection. There is a conversational lyric "yéra mēra" (why dont you fear) (Rāgam: Dési, Tālam: Ādi) between Līlāvati, Prahlāda and Hiranyakasipu. After this there is again a punishment meted out to Prahlāda by the demons, which is followed by surprise, persuasion, and devotion, etc. Prahlāda when thrown into the fire prays to Lord Narayana in hymnical verses, which are followed by conversation between Prahlāda and Hiranyakasipu after which Prahlāda is again handed over to Chanda and Amarka. A scene of Prahlāda preaching bhakti to other students in the hermit school follows. This involves a bhajan like lyrical singing involving chorus. The teachers punish other students and not Prahlāda and also complain to Hiranyakasipu. Another conversation "veruvavadéra" (why are you not afraid) between Prahlāda and Hiranyakasipu (Rāgam: Janjhūti, Tālam: Ādi) follows. The creation and emergence of the evil spirit Kritti through witchcraft ritual is terrifying "kritti anedu śakti" (a power called kritti) Rāgam: Pharas, Tālam: Chapu).

The boomeranging of Kritti on Chanda and Amarka is described in dwipada verse. When Chanda and Amarka report this to

Hiranyakasipu, he arrogantly and angrily asks Prahlāda who Hari was with "yevadura" (who is that) (Rāgam: Kāmbhōji Tālam: Khandachāpu). Another samvāda daruvu (conversational lyric) amongst Hiranyakasipu, Līlāvati and Prahlāda "nā māta vinavu" (you dont listen to me) (Rāgam: Kédāragoula, Tālam: Misrachāpu) follows. This leads to the climax scene with the conversational lyric between Prahlāda and Hiranyakasipu "ýedirōri" (where is my dear little fellow) (Rāgam: Janjhūti, Tālam: Misrachāpu), which is followed by verses in Telugu and Sanskrit and the climax peaks with the lyric "raveneedu" (come my dear) (Rāgam: Punnāgavarāli, Tālam: Tisrachāpu), which is intervened by hymn like verses (tévārams) sung in high pitch, followed by another devotional lyric "saranantini karunimpumu" (I surrender (to you) please be kind to me) (Rāgam: Sourāshtra, Tālam: Ādi Samayati). The following lyric "avatarinchenadigo" (Lo there he manifests) describing Narasimha's emergence (Rāgam: Nāta, Samayati) is mixed with horror and devotion. The conversation between Narasimha and Hiranyakasipu runs in verses. The killing of Hiranyakasipu by Narasimha is described in the lyric "dura monarinchiri..."(They faught a battle). Pacification of Narasimha by Prahlāda is done through a lyric "rakshamām..." (Protect me) (Rāgam: Pantuvarāli, Tālam: Misra Chāpu), which concludes in a Sanskrit slōka and Telugu verse. The performance ends with a mangalam (Plate-XXIV) in Bhairavi Rāgam "mangalam Nrisimha," (all the best to Narasimha), which infuses the mood with a serene coolness. Since today's Kūchipūdi Prahlāda Charitra Nātakam is a shortened version of the above-described traditional performance, it involves only a few of the above rasa elements and lyrics.

Mélattūr Performance

As mentioned in the previous chapter, the Mélattūr performance begins with the episode of Sukracharya reminding Hiranyakasipu (Plate-XXV) of the death of Hiranyaksha.

This episode begins with the prose narration by Sukracharya, "sahajuni champinavairi..."(Enemy who killed your brother). The mood of the narrative is neutral here. To this Hiranyakasipu reacts

Plate-XXIII: Katikamvādu (the baton holder) of Mélattūr Prahlāda Nātakam, the raised fist is to mime the holding.

Plate-XXIV: The last scene of Kūchipūdi Prahlāda Nātakam, Mangalam Nrisimha: Sacred circling of camphor lamp to cool down the ferocious God.

with a frantic shout "Hiranyaksha..." (Plate-XXVI) with aguish and anger mixed with pathos. At this juncture, Līlāvati tries to cool down Hiranyakasipu through her lyric "intākōpamēmīra..." (Why such anger my dear) (Rāgam: Nādanāmakriya: Tālam: Ādi). This turns into a Samvāda daruvu (conversational) between Līlāvati and Hiranyakasipu. Hiranyakasipu's replies are arrogant and full of vīra (valorous zeal) rasa (Plate-XXVII). When Līlāvati is disappointed there is a lyric "Hari nīmīdi vairambu..." (Vishnu my enmity with you) (Rāgam: Dhanyāsi, Tālam: Ādi) ringing out the mood of vexation born out of disappointment. Hiranyakasipu replies through verses (usually rendered like prose by Mélattūr performers) "Cheliyaro Nēvéla chinta" (my sweet heart why do you worry) in a mood of sringara (romance) laced with arrogance and vīra. Hiranyakasipu then orders his demon soldiers to search for Lord Vishnu and trouble all the devotees of the Lord. At this juncture, the lyric "Hiranyakasipudégenō..." (Here goes Hiranyakasipu) (Tālam: Tripuṭa) sets in a mood of Bhayanaka (horror). But, interestingly, this lyric runs in medium pace. It probably suggests the timidity of the demon soldiers and thus adds a dash of humour, which dilutes the horror inherent in the episode. The demon soldiers return to Hiranyakasipu and report (through narrative prose) that they searched for Lord Vishnu but in vain. Hiranyakasipu orders them to go back and continue the search. The episode depicts both the anger of Hiranyakasipu and also the humour generated by the demon soldiers. Prahlāda then tries to persuade his father to give up his enmity with Lord Vishnu.

The verse and prose mixed in his speech creates a mood of Santa. The entry of Chandāmarka, the son of Sukracharya[1] who is asked to impart demonical education to Prahlāda at this juncture is humorous and there after the instruction to Prahlāda runs in a humorous vein. Significantly, Chandāmarka is depicted as a low type comic character. After this, Chandāmarka hands Prahlāda over to his father. Here, the conversation between Prahlāda and Hiranyakasipu is in prose. Hiranyakasipu expresses his Vātsalya (parental affection) in the beginning and Prahlāda exhibits devotion for Lord Vishnu. Gradually Hiranyakasipu experiences disappointment, vexation and anger and finally charges at Prahlāda ferociously. Līlāvati at this juncture tries to pacify Hiranyakasipu and implores him to exhibit compassion for the small child. Līlāvati performs various sancharis (Transitory emotions) to the long lyric "chinni bāludu..." (little lad) which is predominant with pathos mixed with parental affection and nostalgia, as the childhood of Prahlāda is recounted. This gradually leads to another lyric "yémani tāludu" (how can I withstand) (Rāgam: Āhiri, Tālam: Ādi), with an intensely pathetic mood during which Līlāvati resorts to several frantic expressions of hysteric impulse of helplessness. Prahlāda consoles his mother in a Santa frame of mind (this is done through miming). This is followed by a sequence of scenes of punishment meted out to Prahlāda. The sequence of moods during these scenes is almost identical to that of the scenes of Kūchipūdi Prahlāda Charitra Nātakam. This is followed immediately by a conversation between Prahlāda and Hiranyakasipu during which the anger of Hiranyakasipu is replaced with helplessness and amazement.

After Hiranyakasipu asks Prahlāda to show Lord Vishnu the performance suddenly shifts away from the stage into the audience, as the performers descend from the stage and walk through the audience (Plates-XXVIII & XXIX). Here, Prahlāda renders a long devotional lyric as he goes around the stage. Significantly, Prahlāda does not give any lip movement and thus the lyric is shown to be only a meditation of Prahlāda. With this the mood of the performance turns extremely devotional and ritualistic. At this juncture (Plate-XXX), Hiranyakasipu breaks the pillar and Narasimha crashes out of the pillar. Hiranyakasipu delivers a long monologue (prose) during which Narasimha's ferocious mood is kept under control with the help of a few team members who clip Narasimha from all sides stopping him from moving forward (Plate-XXXI) (As mentioned in the second chapter, this is resorted to prevent any untoward action by Narasimha role player). At this juncture, Hiranyakasipu thanks Prahlāda for having facilitated the long awaited encounter with his enemy. This expression of Hiranyakasipu has a suggestion of devotion. Hiranyakasipu praises

Prahlāda as a great devotee in lofty words and sends him off the scene. Narasimha ridicules Hiranyakasipu for troubling a boy of his own community. Hiranyakasipu in turn heckles at the awkwardness of Narasimha's form. Narasimha is so intensely ferocious that he is required to be held back strongly by the group of performance assistants. Probably, that is the reason why the scene of Hiranyakasipu getting killed by Narasimha is deleted by the Mélattūr team now-a-day. This is immediately followed by the scene of Narasimha being worshiped just as any idol in a temple (Plate-VIII). Here, lyrics are sung in chorus to pacify Narasimha's ferociousness. Narasimha cools down and a ritualistic devotional atmosphere is established when Pānakam, the sweet water made out of Jaggery, is distributed among the audience. The Narasimha mask is taken back in a procession to its place (Plate-XXXII) in the temple and with this the performance comes to an end.

The sequence of moods in the portions common to Kūchipūdi and Mélattūr is almost similar. The significant difference lies in the exaggeration of the moods found in the Mélattūr performance (Plates-XXXIII, XXXV & XXXVII) and the contrasting balance of moods maintained in the Kūchipūdi performance (Plates- XXXIV, XXXVI & XXXVIII). The frantic anger of Hiranyakasipu, the hysteric pathos of Līlāvati (Plate-XXXIX) and uncontrollable ferociousness of Narasimha characterize the melodramatic expressions of the Mélattūr performance. The following prose dialogues of Hiranyakasipu exemplify the melodramatic content of the Mélattūr performance:

Dialogue–1

"Cheliyarō .... cheliyarō nēvéla chinta nondévu ah ha ha

Cheliyarō nēvéla chinta nondévu ....

ilalōna tana balamberugavā yanchu nēku teliyalédā

tana vīra sūra parākrama mantayū teliyaléda.... ah... ha... ha...

kondalu chendādudun cheliyā, kondalu chendādudun

kondalu chendādi pindi...pindi... gāvintunu ....

badabāgni kannīru pāpakīdagunā..........................

kadimi pravāhambu kadali ka dagunā ....

mahinalla pōtulu mattēbha mounā ....

rahinalla pakshulu rāhamsa mounā ....

Cheliyarō.... rahinalla pakshulu rāhamsa mounā ....

yenta mātrambu...yeh...yeh...yeh...yeh...yeh ....

yenta mātrambu....yī .... indirā vibhudu ....

kāntarō .... nanumīri kadalirālēdu ....

kāntarō nanumīri kadali ralēdu telusunā ....

nanumīri kadalirālēdu ....

pāgārikainā....āparamēshtikaina...

kayyāna viduvadu .... ayya... yya...yya...yya...yyo

nīvitula ā .... la...pada..valadu ....

cheliyarō .... vinave ...... munupu nēnu

ā Harini chūsi .... āhāramulumāni!... ahamu tolaginchi....

apudu vanajasambhavudu nāku varamichhinādu...eh..eh..eh

āyudambunanainā .... astramunanainā...

vēyichupulanainā.... vēlpulanainā....

pāmula pasumriga pakshulanainā ....

chimatō modalagu jantuvulanainā ....

pagalambunainā.... rātrulanainā ....

jagatilō nendunanu ..eh..eh..eh..eh..eh ....

chāvulēdanu varamulu gaikonti....cheliyā.... telusunā

idinīku...teliya lédā ....

cāvulēdanu varamugaikontini ....

nēnu ā Harini cūda .... celiyaro ....

nēnu ā Harini cūda....kanulā kanadu ā souri...

ipudē rāsasula nampi ....

ā panka..dasuni madamana ginceda ....

The above dialogue may be translated as follows:

Sweet heart ……..Sweet heart

Why do you worry ah…ha…ha …

Sweet heart

Why do you worry?

Don't you know my strength amongst the people of the world?

Did not you realize …….

All my valour, fears, might, do you not realize….ah…

I can play with mountains like balls my sweet heart, I can play with mountains

Playing balls with mountain

I can crush them into powder

Is it right to give oceanic fire through tears to your eye balls

Is it right to make this flow of tears into a sea

Can a black buffalo be an elephant?

Can any common bird be a royal swan?

Sweat heart can any common bird be a royal swan

What a friendship ah... ha…ha…

What a friendship yi…yi…yi…

Lord Indra

Woman.........

Cannot come surpassing me

Woman cannot come crossing over me do you know

Do you know?

Cannot come going against me

I would not leave one even Lord Vishnu or even Brahma... yi…yi…

You don't this way lament …

sweet heart … listen once

Beholding Lord Vishnu giving up food shedding my ego

Then the creator God, Lord Brahma sanctioned a boon to me…eh…eh…

Either with a weapon, or with a magical power, or with a thousand eyes, or by gods, or from snakes, or animals, or birds, or from animals ranging from ant, either during day time, or during night, at any place in the world … eh… eh…

There is no death to me, such a boon I received, sweet heart, do you know

Did you not know this?

No death to me, such a boon I did receive

When I tried to see Lord Vishnu, my sweet heart, when I tried to see Lord Vishnu, my sweet heart … he does not appear to me

Right now, will I send my demon soldiers and bring down the arrogance of that slave

Dialogue–2

eh…eh....eh.... Hiranyāksha āh…ha…ha…ha ....

Hiranyāksha .... Hiranyāksha ....

Hari nā vairi.... vinavayya ....

vinavayya …guruvayya....vipula Talamuna ....

tana sahodaruni .... eh…eḥ...eh…

tana sahōdaruni champina sourini viduvā ....

pā..tā..lamuna vādu pā..ri..pō..yinādu....yeh…eh…

yētenchi....yētenchi kanugāna yandudāginādu ....

konchāna viduvanu...ah..ah..ah..ah...ah..ēkolayambunan.

vanchimpa .... naché.. vadhiyimpabadu ....

nī....katākshamuna .... sadgurō .... nī..katākshamuna...

vedakinchi .... Harini .... ooh...ooh...ooh ....

chīkāku parchedanū....sī....gra....me....ipudū ....

The above dialogue may be translated as follows:

Eh … eh … eh … Hiranyākshaaa …. Hiranyākshaaa ….

Vishnu is my enemy … listen

Listen my Guru, on the wide surface of the earth … my brother's … eh …

My brother's killer Vishnu, I would not leave

He ran away to the world outside the earth … eh…

Descending descending

He hid himself making himself invisible

I will not leave him, as simple as that wherever he hides … āh … hā… hā…

Deceived by me … he will get killed

With your blissful grace, my great Guru

With your blissful grace

Searching for him … Vishnu … ooh …

I will frustrate him … soon at once now

Dialogue–3

āh...āh,,,āh. .āh. .āh....āh…āh ....

āh...āh,,, āh..āh..āh—āh...āh ....

vinu vārijākshiro ....

yī vīdu .... durmadhudu ....

manakula hāni kāvincha puttinādu ....

kutila chittudu ....vīdu....daityakula bāndhavudu

ka...ta...ka...tā....ituvanti kān....tu...du...manakū …

lélé .... ga...manaku...vī...dendu...ga..li..gé …

vinu vārijākshiro …

kodukāni yenchanu kommaro....kodukāni yenchanu.

vīnini pudamilō adhamanagintunu vé...ga....mé
āh...āh...āh....āh

The above dialogue may be translated as follows:

Ah … ah … ah …

Listen, the beautiful eyed one!

This fellow…. badly proud …

Is born with the purpose of damaging our lineage

Crooked hearted … this fellow … the kith of the demon race

Alas … this kind of son to us after a long wait for issues … to us … how is this fellow born

Listen, the lotus-eyed one,

I consider this fellow as my son … I did consider this fellow as my son

This fellow now here, I will humble soon at once, ah … ah …

Plate-XXV: Sahajuni Champina Vairi: dialogue rendered by Sukracharya reminding the death of Hiranyaksha to Hiranyakasipu as Līlāvati and Prahlāda watch on, in Mélattūr Prahlāda Nātakam.

Plate-XXVI: Hiranyakasipu reacts with a frantic shout "Hiranyaksha..." when Sukracharya reminding the death of Hiranyaksha in the Mélattūr Prahlāda Nātakam.

Plate-XXVII: Hiranyākshaaaa: In Mélattūr Prahlāda Nātakam Hiranyakasipu cries in anger as Līlāvati is afraid and Prahlāda is amazed.

Plate-XXVIII: Mélattūr Prahlāda Nātakam shifts into the audience. Hiranyakasipu is challenging Prahlāda to show Narasimha, as both of them face the stage. A view from the stage.

Plate-XXIX: Mélattūr Prahlāda Nātakam shifts into the audience. Hiranyakasipu is satirically commenting on the shape of Narasimha on the stage. A view from the stage.

Plate-XXX: The climax scene from Mélattūr Prahlāda Nātakam. Hiranyakasipu facing the stage from the ground about to break the pillar on the stage as Prahlāda who inspired the act watches on standing beside him.

Plate-XXXI: Narasimha of Mélattūr Prahlāda Nātakam rushing forward ferociously overpowering the performance assistants holding him.

Plate-XXXII: Narasimha mask of Mélattūr Prahlāda Nātakam being taken in procession to Varadaraja Perumal temple towards the end of the performance.

Plate-XXXIII: A scene from Mélattūr Prahlāda Nātakam. Hiranyakasipu is irritated to see Prahlāda praising lord Vishnu, when asked to demonstrate his learning at the school. Note the exaggeration in Hiranyakasipu's expression.

Plate-XXXIV: A scene from Kūchipūḍi Prahlāda Nātakam. Hiranyakasipu is trying to ascertain the learning of Prahlāda at School. Note the cool and balanced expression.

Plate-XXXV: A scene from Mélattūr Prahlāda Nātakam. Hiranyakasipu claims his invincible strength as part of the entry lyric. Note the emphatic expression.

Plate-XXXVI: A scene from Kūchipūdi Prahlāda Nātakam Hiranyakasipu claims his invincible strength as part of the entry lyric. Note the balanced expression.

Plate-XXXVII: A scene from Mélattūr Prahlāda Nātakam. Hiranyakasipu angry with Prahlāda for his obstinacy in devotion for lord Vishnu pushes him off from his lap. Note the emphatic expression.

Plate-XXXVIII: A scene from Kūchipūdi Prahlāda Nātakam. Hiranyakasipu gets angry with Prahlāda for his obstinacy in devotion to lord Vishnu and moves off from him. Note the balanced expression.

These dialogues are uttered by Hiranyakasipu in a typically Mélattūr style of saying a word following by a pause before the next word is uttered in raised voice in an artificially rhetorical tone, typical to Mélattūr performance. Another distinctive feature of the dialogue delivery is the strong and powerful cries, hissing, gasping, etc., as seen in the above example which includes the usage of sounds close to the cry of an animal, which give an effect of demonical roughness.

Another example of exaggerated presentation in Mélattūr Prahlāda Charitra Nātakam may be seen in Līlāvati's hysteric convulsions in the context of Prahlāda's punishment. In this scene, Līlāvati beats her chest, weeps and sobs, cries, gasps, stoops and falls on the ground, runs on the stage fervently shaking and shuddering, as if in a trance and attempts to commit suicide before she is stopped by a gentle Prahlāda.

Yet another example of intensely emphatic enactment of extreme emotions, which characterise Mélattūr Prahlāda Charitra Nātakam, is found in the presentation of the Narasimha character. Narasimha after crashing out of the pillar swings back and forth and displays uncontrollable ferociousness as if possessed by a cosmic destructive power out to destroy everything in the world. His gasping, shaking, shivering, swinging, forging, etc., the performance assistants controlling the Narasimha performer by holding him tight and restraining him from all sides as he forges ahead, trying to escape from the people overpowering him, etc., make the Narasimha presentation intensely emphatic. Chandāmarka, Prahlāda's instructor is portrayed as a comic character and an element of humour is attributed to the antagonist characters like the demon soldiers and an attempt is made to heckle at them.

Thus we may see that the presentation of the characters in the Mélattūr Prahlāda Charitra Nātakam is marked by an over emphasis of certain features and emotions. This is also evident in the costume and the body movements used in the Mélattūr Prahlāda Charitra Nātakam. The masks used for demons reinforce the larger than life demonical images of these soldiers (Plate-XL).

Even the mask of the Narasimha is asymmetrically bigger than the real head of lion and human being. In fact, it is not in proportion with the size of the body of the actor playing the Narasimha role. The mask is almost 3 feet in diameter and is designed to be emphatically ferocious and horrifying (Plate-XLI). At the same time, it is glorified and considered sacred (Plates-V, VI).

Even the costume of the Hiranyakasipu is also glorified and larger than life. The gait and the body movements of Hiranyakasipu in the way he bends backwards or to the side or stretches his hands in highly emphatic manner (Plate-XLII). His gait is emphatic with the foot raised from the ground strongly and, after a strange movement of the foot, put down powerfully. These movements are probably meant to emphasise the demonic nature of Hiranyakasipu (Plate-XLIII).

In all the above aspects of character presentation, Kūchipūdi Prahlāda Charitra Nātakam is marked by features different from Mélattūr. For example, Hiranyakasipu's costume in Kūchipūdi Prahlāda Charitra Nātakam is like that of any emperor. The body movements of Hiranyakasipu do not reflect any extra human quality. Demon soldiers in Kūchipūdi Prahlāda Charitra Nātakam do wear masks. The demon soldiers with human faces are as frightening as they are imagined to be.

The Narasimha mask in Kūchipūdi Prahlāda Charitra Nātakam has no emphatic design as the Mélattūr one (Plate-XLIV). Līlāvati's behaviour is never emphatic beyond a limit (Plate-XLV, XLVI). While persuading Prahlāda to follow his father's orders (Plate-XLVII) and in other scenes full of pathos she maintains the norms of sophistication worthy of an empress. Because of her attempt to maintain balance within certain limits, the humour in the instruction of Prahlāda by Chanda and Amarka also does not go beyond a certain limit and does not remove the image of learnedness of Chanda and Amarka. Theirs is a scholarly humour. Though the Narasimha performer of Kūchipūdi Prahlāda Charitra Nātakam is said to have been possessed by Lord Narasimha in the past, today the character Narasimha is ferocious but not possessed.

Plate-XXXIX: A scene from Mélattūr Prahlāda Nātakam. Līlāvati's hysteric wailing as Hiranyakasipu decides to punish Prahlāda.

Plate-XL: Mélattūr demon soldiers expressing response to scolding by Hiranyakasipu for having failed in locating lord Vishnu. Note: The clown like expression.

Plate-XLI: Worship of Narasimha dancer in Mélattūr Prahlāda Nātakam as Sutradhara recites hymns. Note the out of proportion size of the mask.

Plate-XLII: Mélattūr Hiranyakasipu part of the dance to the lyric which he claims his invincible strength. Note the emphatic expression.

Plate-XLIII: Mélattūr Hiranyakasipu's facial expression emphasising horrifying cruelty.

Plate-XLIV: Kūchipūdi Narasimha engaged in a conversation with Hiranyakasipu. Note: The Narasimha mask has a naturalistic design. (Source: Mr. Shard B. Pitti)

Plate-XLV: A scene from Kuchipudi Prahlada Natakam. Note Lilavathi coolly patting Prahlada as Hiranyakasipu claims his invincible strength.

Plate-XLVI: A scene from Kūchipūdi Prahlāda Nātakam. Note Līlāvati expressing her balance amazement at the unstinting devotion of her young son.

As observed in the earlier part of the chapter, the scenes, conversations, lyrics and monologues are all long in Mélattūr Prahlāda Charitra Nātakam. Thus, each emotion is to be sustained for a long time and, also, the emotion is built gradually during this long performance. For example, the convulsion of Līlāvati, which is totally absent in Kūchipūdi Prahlāda Charitra Nātakam, runs for an abnormal time in Mélattūr Prahlāda Charitra Nātakam. Similarly, the Narasimha character, who in any Prahlāda Charitra Nātakam performance, including Kūchipūdi Prahlāda Charitra Nātakam, does not take much time in stooping over Hiranyakasipu and killing him, in the Mélattūr performance stays ferocious for an unusually long time sustaining his anger with the same intensity for all this period. In fact, in Mélattūr Prahlāda Charitra Nātakam the stooping and killing scene is completely avoided. Comparatively in Kūchipūdi Prahlāda Charitra Nātakam scenes are shorter, each emotion is sustained for a short time and the rasās are built up as a part of this process of a quick change of emotions.

ĀNGIKĀBHINAYAM

Though the Kūchipūdi and Mélattūr dance traditions have been recognised to be similar in several details, the Āngikābhinayam (the enactment through body language of dance tradition) in Kūchipūdi and Mélattūr Prahlāda Charitra Nātakam is to be more meticulously compared to identify the similarities and differences between the two. If Āngikābhinayam in both is found to be similar it is basically because of adopting the norms of Nātya Sāstra in both the styles. Another basis of similarity in these two performances is the flexibility of movement because of which the traditions were identified as folk rather than classical.

When observed meticulously, Mélattūr Āngikābhinayam, as found in Prahlāda Charitra Nātakam, shows the influence of the Tamil tradition of Indian classical dance, which is now known as Bharatanātyam. An evidence of this influence is seen in the Tērmānams (ending method of each piece of abhinayam). It is also called Muktāyi/Tērmānam and has a feature of the same body movement being rendered thrice.

Figure-III shows one of the well-known varieties of Tērmānams found in Bharatanātyam, which is also seen in Mélattūr performances. During this movement, as is the norm in Bharatanātyam, legs remain in the 'aramandi' (half sitting dance position) position and the footwork is according to the mnemonic syllables. It goes without saying that the rule of "yetōhasta statōdrishtihi" takes the head and the eyes along with the palm. The second most well-known Tērmānam of Bharatanātyam, which is also seen in Mélattūr performance, is as shown in figure IV. The Kūchipūdi performers are never found to be executing these Tērmānams. Interestingly, these Tērmānams are executed frequently in Mélattūr Prahlāda Charitra Nātakam.

Another feature of Bharatanātyam found in Mélattūr Prahlāda Charitra Nātakam is the movement of the body above the waist, less flexible as compared to the same in the Kūchipūdi performance. In the Kūchipūdi body language the legs do not remain stiff as in Bharatanātyam. In Kūchipūdi dance, the leg bends and unbends sidewise at the knee to swing the upper torso to the rhythm of the mridangam (percussion instrument) syllables or the lyric. The body movement in Kūchipūdi is very flexible and swing is used at times to shift the weight on the foot from one direction to the other with the throw of the upper torso in a small angle from the vertically stiff, perpendicular line maintained in Bharatanātyam (Figures-V, VI).

This sometimes results in the throwing of the head back and forth with the rhythm of the syllables or the lyric (Figures-V, VI). In the Mélattūr Prahlāda Charitra Nātakam these typically Kūchipūdi body-swings are not found.

CHOREOGRAPHY

An important similarity between Bharatanātyam and Mélattūr Prahlāda Charitra Nātakam performance is 'padārdhābhinaya' found in the two dance performances. In the Kūchipūdi dance performance the choreography takes into account the total import of each sentence, and the meaning of each and every word in the sentence is not depicted. On the other hand, in the Bharatanātyam tradition, the meaning of every word in the sentence is depicted through abhinaya. This feature is found in Mélattūr Prahlāda Charitra Nātakam performance also. The Mélattūr performance has been exemplified in the figures through the lyric "inta kopa mémira swami" inta = this much (Figure-VIIa) kopamu = anger (Figure-VIIb) yemira= why my dear (Figure-VIIc) swamy = Lord/husband (Figure-VIId) swamy = Lord (Figure-VIIe),

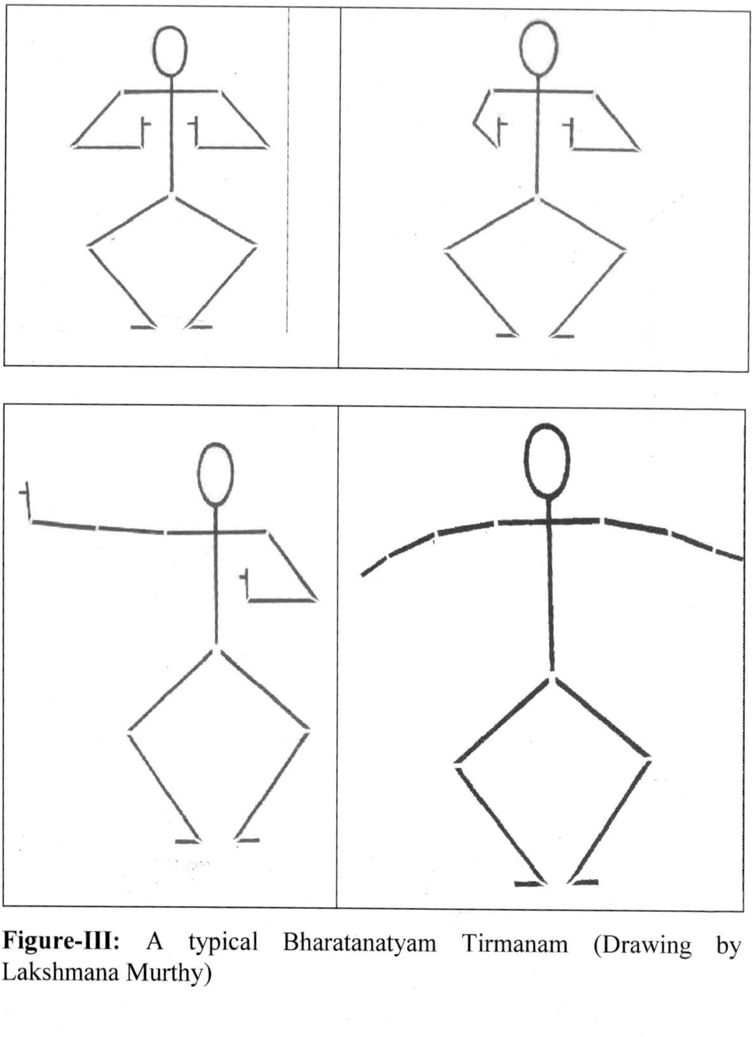

Figure-III: A typical Bharatanatyam Tirmanam (Drawing by Lakshmana Murthy)

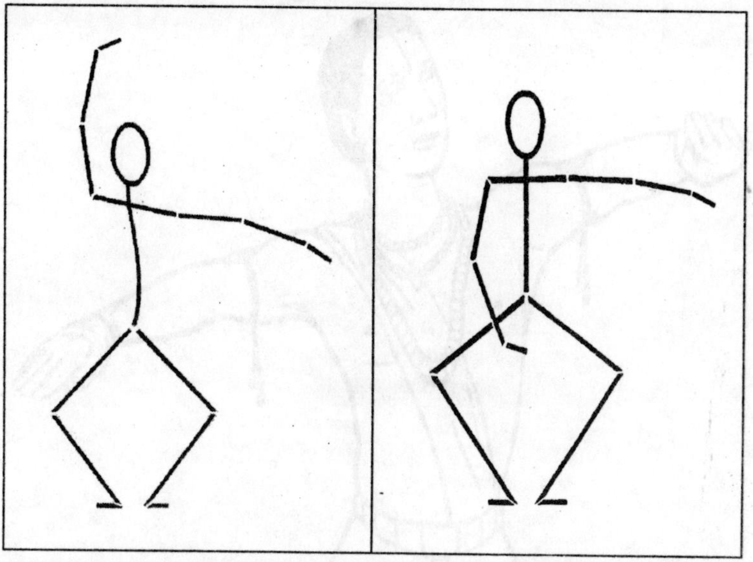

Figure-IV: Another typical Bharatanātyam Tērmānam (Drawing by Lakshmana Murthy)

Interestingly, Mélattūr Prahlāda Charitra Nātakam performance has a feature of Kūchipūdi dance, namely the abhinaya of sancharis, which is found in the Tarangam and other performances of the Kūchipūdi tradition. But abhinaya of sancharis is not found in the Kūchipūdi Prahlāda Charitra Nātakam performance. Probably, this has got to do with the attempt to quicken the pace of the Kūchipūdi Prahlāda Charitra Nātakam performance in contrast to leisurely performance found in Mélattūr Prahlāda Charitra Nātakam. A good example of abhinaya of the sancharis in Mélattūr Prahlāda Charitra Nātakam is found in the performance of Līlāvati's lyric "chinni bāludu". For the one phrase "chinni bāludu" (little lad) Līlāvati enacts a variety of rural children's games played by Prahlāda in his early childhood.

MUSIC COMPONENT

Music in the Mélattūr Prahlāda Charitra Nātakam performance can be clearly identified as close to the Pāta Kachéri (singing concert) tradition, which is marked by gradual development of swara sancharas and intense repetition of lines with various swara compositions

Figure-V: Typical Kūchipūdi Āngikābhinayam. Note the flexibility of the movement (Drawing by Lakshmana Murthy)

Figure-VI: Typical Kūchipūdi Āngikābhinayam. Note the flexibility of the movement. (Drawing by Lakshmana Murthy)

Figure-VII: *(a) Inta* = This much

(b) Kopamu = Anger

(c) Yemira = why my dear

(d) Swami = Lord/husband.

(e) Swami = Lord.

with a stress on music rather than what is being conveyed in the lyric, etc. Music in the Kūchipūdi Prahlāda Charitra Nātakam performance belongs to Ata Kachéri (dance concerts) tradition, which is marked by quick sanchara of swaras, less repetitions and stress on what is being conveyed in the lyric rather than on the musical skill. The Mélattūr music composition for the lyrics does not involve Gati bhédas but a change of Kālams (speeds) is demonstrated on each lyric towards the end. In the Kūchipūdi music composition each lyric is composed incorporating the Gati bhédas in the singing of the lyric itself.

The major Ragas used by the Mélattūr team (Plate-XLVIII) are Nādanāmakriya, Janjhūti and Yaman Kalyāni. Interestingly, all these ragas exhibit a common quality: that of being Madhyama shruti ragas, i.e., all these ragas run between Nishāda and Nishāda. For this reason, these ragas suit to a serene devotional mood[2]. These ragas, along with Punnāgavarāli, Dévagāndhāri and Āhiri, are all vakra ragas, i.e., the patterns of Ārohana (ascending) and Avarōhana (descending) are not similar. If Ārohana has the normal order of notes from Sa to Ni, Avarōhana may have a non-normal order of notes or vice-versa. Because of these complicated note restrictions these ragas are generally avoided in concerts[3]. Only the orthodox musicians prefer to deal with these ragas. The occurrence of these ragas in the Mélattūr Prahlāda Charitra Nātakam compositions indicates the inclination of the Mélattūr team towards orthodoxy even in terms of music. Regarding the devotional quality of ragas like Dévagāndhāri, an interesting fact of Mélattūr Prahlāda Charitra Nātakam performance needs a special mention.

The Pravesa Daruvu "kaduvadinādu chuda yédi" (entry lyric) for Hiranyakasipu is sung in Dévagāndhāri rāgam, that too in a devotional tone, though the ferociousness of Hiranyakasipu is manifest only in the enactment by the performer playing the Hiranyakasipu role. It may be noted here that it is in Dévagāndhari that Tyagaraja composed the famous kirtana "Kshīrasāgara sayana".

In the Kūchipūdi Prahlāda Charitra Nātakam performance the set of ragas used cannot be classified into a special category on the basis of any particular salient features. However, the above-mentioned ragas also form a part of the Kūchipūdi Prahlāda Charitra Nātakam. The Kūchipūdi teams prefer the Rakti ragas (ragas to which one gets attracted to immediately).

As has already been mentioned the orthodoxy of the Pāta Kachéri style of singing the Vakra ragas is not found in the Kūchipūdi Prahlāda Charitra Nātakam performance even when the same Vakra ragas are used. This is exemplified in the following notation-wise representation of the musical renderings of three lyrics each of Kūchipūdi and Mélattūr:

Mélattūr Lyric: Music Notation

Pallavi:

Song no.1: Rāgam: Bégada. Tālam: Ādi (chowka kālam)

; ni ṙi sā; ni sā pa dā pā;|

; gā……nā; pa…….tī………..;|

; dā pā;| gā, ma pā mā dā; pā;||

; vāché; | chū.......................dā,ré, ||

8 to 10 times

Anupallvi:

; dā; pā; pā; mā; dā pā mā gā|
; bhakti to;...................|

; gā ma pa ga ma ri gā, ma pā ma | .... mi...................j

pā; mā; dā; pā | |; | |
ri; ro ....||;||

Translation of the above lyric:
(O dear all behold with devotion here comes Ganésh)

Song no.2: Rāgam: Dévagandhāri, Tālam: Ādi.

Pallvi:

; ma, pa, da, pa, ma ga ri ma ga ma ri |
; ka, dū, vā, di nā nu ju ....|

; ri ma pa; | ma pa ma pa da ri sa ni da da nT,||pā||
; yē.... d i ; | ....ka

d ū..., | | p ā | | ka d u va d T |

...............................30 times...............................

Song no.3: Rāgam: Nādanāmakriya, Tālam: Ādi.

Pallavi:

; dā; ni;; ni; sā ni sa ri sā sā |
; in..tā..kō; ....pā mu |

; ni, sā ri sā | ni sa ni da ni sa ni da ||
; yē .mi .... | rā..........sā...........mi||

...............................15 times...............................

Anupallavi:

; pā dā ni sā ni dā pā da ni da pa mā gā mā;|
;i..la lo.............nā ....gā lā;|

; gā, ma pā , mā pā ; mā dā | pā ||
; vai.................ru ; . . la | .... ||

Translation of the above lyric:

(Why my dear such an anger (why are you so angry my dear)

Kūchipūdi Lyrics: Music Notation

Song no.1: Rāgam: Mōhana, Tālam: Ādi (Madhyama kālam):

Pallavi:

;, sā sa sa sa ri ga ri | gā, pa |ri sa sa ||
;,tāndava nrityaka | rī, ga |jā na na ||

;, ga ga ga ga pa pa pa pa |
;, dhimi ki ta dhimi ki ta |

; ga pā da dā | pa da sa da pā ;||
; sou . ri mri | dan............gā ||

Translation of the above lyric:

The elephant headed one, the one who dances vigorously

Song no. 2: Rāgam: Athāna, Tālam: Misra gati.

Pallavi:

,pā gā ma ma || pa pā sā sā ||
,nindu ko lu || vaiyu nnādé ||

,sa sa ga ma ri | sa ri sa ni sā ||
,nikhi lā....ki | rtiga nnā . .dé ||

Anupallavi:

, sā ga ma ri | | sa ni pa gā | |
dandī... tā || ri pu daityu ||

ri;, pā || dā ni ri sa pā ||
de;, dā || nā vén dru du ||

Chaturasra gati:

pā; gā ma ma pa pa sā sā |
ni; du ko lu vaiyu nnādé |

,sa sa gā ri | sa ri sa ni sā ||
, ni khilā ki | rtiga nna dé ||

Translation of the above lyric:

Lo here, he holds his full court, the one who acquired fame all over, the demon who punished his enemies the Lord of the demons.

Song no.3: Rāgam: Mukhāri, Tālam: Misra nadaka,

,pa da sā sā || ni dā pa ma ga ri ||
,va la du rā || . . . ya . . .nna ||

sa ri mā ga ri || ma mā mā mā ||
,va la dū rā .. | | ha ri bhakti | |

Translation of the above lyric:

No my dear no more devotion to Vishnu

Plate-XLVII: A scene from Kūchipūdi Prahlāda Nātakam. Note Līlāvati trying to persuade Prahlāda through counselling (Source: Mr. Shard B. Pitti, Chairman and M.D. Pitti Laminations Hyderabad)

Plate-XLVIII: The Mélattūr music team sit to the right side of the stage (Left of the audience).

It may be observed in the above represented musical renderings that the Mélattūr Prahlāda Charitra Nātakam performance has the musical component very close to a Patakacceri (singing concert), as is found in "Ganapathi vaché" the ālapana between the two syllables *to* and *mi* in the line "bhaktitō mīrirō" is as long as 16 strokes of Ādi Tālam. Each line is repeated many times. The Nritta enactment for this musical rendering notwithstanding, the singing alone stands out as a perfect singing concert. Whereas, in the Kūchipūdi tradition, as is found in the musical rendering of the lyric, "tāndava nrityakarī gajānana", there are no long pauses of ālapana. Though a few repetitions are seen in many other lyrics such as "nindūkoluvaiyunnādé" repetitions are less in number. The meaning of the words rendered becomes significant with smaller or no pauses. In other words, the musical rendering orients itself towards the dance performance rather than the other way round, which is the case in Mélattūr musical rendering. In the Kūchipūdi musical rendering literature is intensely spread through the singing, whereas in the Mélattūr musical rendering it is diluted into a pure music ālapana. This Pāta Kachéri style of musical rendering is more pronounced because of the slōkam type of rendering of few words before the beginning of the rhythmic rendering of a few lyrics. Even in this aspect of musical rendering, Mélattūr Prahlāda Charitra Nātakam performance is close to Bharatanātyam.

An important musical feature in which there is a contrast between Mélattūr and Kūchipūdi performances is the presence or absence of gati shift. Like in any other Kūchipūdi performance, in the Kūchipūdi Prahlāda Charitra Nātakam the gati shifts are introduced into the singing or a lyric without altering the meaning of the words. For example, the above notationally represented lyric "nindūkoluvaiyunnādé..." each repetition is rendered in a different gati.

The first rendering is in Misrachāpu Tālam, and then the first repetition is done in tisram and the second in chaturasram (Ādi). This shift from one gati to the other is smooth and thrills the audience when imitated in the execution of dance. In the Mélattūr Prahlāda Charitra Nātakam performance the variation in rendering is affected only in terms of the kālam (time for given number of notes).

The Mélattūr Prahlāda Charitra Nātakam musical rendering usually begins in chowka kālam (slower range of speed) and continues in the same pace throughout but the dancer executes the steps in all the three speeds from slower to medium and the faster range of speed. It requires an informed audience to appreciate the thrill in the gati bhéda technique adopted by the Mélattūr team. Interestingly, the audience of the Mélattūr Prahlāda Charitra Nātakam performance seems to have this training as part of the general culture of the Tanjore region of Tamil Nadu. The gati shift technique adopted by the Kūchipūdi team is catchy and entertains all kinds and levels of audience. This nature of the gati shift technique is responsible for the technique being adopted in the popular bhajan tradition. Tarangams of the Kūchipūdi repertoire, which belong to the bhajan tradition also, have this gati shift as one of the characteristic features. Similarly, while the singer in the Mélattūr performance continues to sing in the same gati throughout, the dancer executes all the five jatis (chaturasra, tisra, khanda, misra and sankīrna, respectively) in footwork. Also, the Mélattūr performer executes one gati, say chaturasram (4), while the singer continues in a different gati, say misram (7). This is done only for a line or two towards the end of a lyric. But these two gati bhédas performed by the Mélattūr performers are as thrilling and fast as the shift followed by the Kūchipūdi performer along with the gati shift rendered by the singer.

The Kūchipūdi performers, in fact, display the skill of speed variation in rhythm and gati bhéda as the Mélattūr performers do along with their execution of gati shift in footwork, following the same rendered by the singer in singing. But the speed variation in the Kūchipūdi tradition is limited to a variation of three speeds as they usually begin at madhyama (medium range), whereas the possibility of speed variation in Mélattūr is in all the three speeds as they usually begin at chowka kālam (slower range of speed). This is what makes the Mélattūr performance enjoyable. The Kūchipūdi musical rendering is different from Mélattūr musical rendering even in the aspect of kālam because Kūchipūdi musical rendering usually begins with madhyama kālam (medium range of speed), unlike the Mélattūr Prahlāda Charitra Nātakam performance, which begins in chowka kālam (slower range of speed). Even in this regard, Mélattūr Prahlāda Charitra Nātakam performance resembles Bharatanātyam performance.

As is well known, the entry of characters in the Kūchipūdi begins with sollukattu jati. If there is a pravesa daruvu (entry lyric) for the entry, the sollukattu is sung generally before the lyric is rendered. This is not found in the entries and exits of the Mélattūr Prahlāda Charitra Nātakam characters. The pravesa daruvu is not compulsory for all the characters other than the main character (who usually makes his/her entry first). The character, which enters subsequent to the main character just walks on to the stage.

Similarly, the exits of characters from the stage are also not compulsorily associated with lyric or sollukattu renderings in Mélattūr Prahlāda Charitra Nātakam. The characters casually walk out of the stage to exit. Lack of lyric or rhythm at the second and later entries of the characters found in both Mélattūr and Bharatanātyam performances may have different reasons. In Mélattūr performance the ritual nature does not demand artistic attraction.

SPEECH CHARACTERISTICS

The Tamil influence found in terms of closeness to Bharatanātyam is also found in the Tamil accent of the Telugu word renderings, both in prose and song, of the Mélattūr Prahlāda Charitra Nātakam. This is as natural as the Kūchipūdi performers using the coastal agrahara Brahmin dialect in terms of accent, and intonation. In fact, the habit of the Tamil speaking Mélattūr performers led to the intonation of any Tamil words and expressions in the prose renderings in the Mélattūr performances, because the performers try to strictly implement the script, which was originally composed without any Tamil influence.[4] But the lack of touch with Telugu speaking environment gets reflected in the prose conversations of the Mélattūr performers in which several verses are also rendered like prose. For example,

"Cheliyarō nīvéla chintanondévu," "ilalōnatanabalamberugavāyanchu"

It is exactly a dwipada verse, which fulfils all the metrical requirements of the dwipada prosody. The Kūchipūdi performers on the other hand render such verses in a typical Yakshagāna style of rendering verses using differnt Classical Carnatic Ragas. This Kūchipūdi style of rendering verses is different from the style of rendering verses in the pourānika Nātakams of modern times.

The above observations about the Mélattūr performance may be summed up in the following words of Mr. R. Parthasarathy[5]:

> "The sentiments are expressed in classical music of high class carnatic tradition and the dance and abhinaya are in Bhārata Nātya technique and, occasionally with poetic speeches, dialogues and appropriate dramatic action. Abhinaya are more elaborate and incisive."

In contrast, in Kūchipūdi Prahlāda Charitra Nātakam the performance is in a typical Kūchipūdi technique of dance and abhinaya in the Āta kachéri style of carnatic music with less elaborate and less melodramatic abhinaya with a quick moving sequence of things.

REFERENCES

1. Interestingly the Mélattūr version treats Chandamarka as a single person, though Chandamarka is treated as a compound of two names Chanda and Amarka in the Kūchipūdi version. According to Natarajan, this is because of shortage of the performers in the beginning.
2. Interview with Tampella Suryanarayana 15th January 1997.
3. Interview with Tampella Suryanarayana 15th January 1997.
4. Though the script by Mélattūr Venkata Rama Sastry could not be procured, even from the performance text it can be seen that Telugu used in this script is chaste and learned.
5. Parthasarathy R, M.L., "The Unique Features of Mélattūr Bhāgavata Méla Tradition" (A Telugu Heritage in Tamil Nadu) Bhāgavata Méla Nātya Nātakam, a souvneir, Mēlattūr, Sri Laxmi Narasimha Jayanti Bhagavata Méla Nātya Nātaka Sangam, own Publication, Mēlattūr, 1995.

5
Conclusion

The comparison at the macro and micro levels of Kūchipūdi and Mélattūr Prahlāda Charitra Nātakam reveals the predominance of artistic and ritualistic natures in the Kūchipūdi and Mélattūr performances, respectively. The hypothesis drawn on the basis of the survey of the overall repertoires of Kūchipūdi and Mélattūr dance traditions indicate that the apparently similar dance traditions display the demarcation of artistic and ritual orientations, even at the macro and micro levels of a specific dance drama performance, namely Prahlāda Charitra Nātakam. The cultural background of Prahlāda Charitra Nātakam performances discussed in the third chapter clearly establishes a religious and ritualistic background for both Kūchipūdi and Mélattūr Prahlāda Charitra Nātakam performances. However, as observed from the memories of the senior Kūchipūdi performers, it appears that the ritualistic nature of the Kūchipūdi Prahlāda Charitra Nātakam performance gradually got diluted under the influence of professional pressures, which the Kūchipūdi team underwent in course of time. On the other hand, the ritualistic aspect of the Prahlāda Charitra Nātakam performance is continued in Mélattūr tradition. In fact, it is this ritualistic aspect which is preserving and sustaining the Mélattūr dance drama tradition, in which the Prahlāda Charitra Nātakam performance has a prominent ritualistic place.

Here, it is noteworthy to remember that the enthusiasm about classical dance traditions among the general public is only a recent phenomenon in the Indian Society. Under such an atmosphere of new born enthusiasm, the Mélattūr team finds many words and gestures of encouragement from the public. But it is their devotion to Lord Narasimha and their faith in his power that sustained their heritage even in an intense Tamil atmosphere. The analysis in the last two chapters shows that the Tamil environment under which the Mélattūr teams sustained their tradition did not fail to influence the Mélattūr dance tradition.

The dearth of patronage for the art of classical dance and the above described new born enthusiasm had its impact on the Kūchipūdi team, which always sustained on it as a profession for making a living. This impact diluted the ritualistic aspect in the tradition and intensified the artistic aspects, which is one of the main reasons behind the expansion of the repertoire of the Kūchipūdi team as discussed in the second chapter.

The comparative study of the two great classical dance traditions of Kūchipūdi and Mélattūr is in no way exhaustive. But this comparison, it is hoped, highlights the need for a more meticulous comparative study of the two forms, rather than the superficial observation of similarity between the two dance traditions. As was observed in the previous comparative study by C. Ramanadham, even in case of Prahlāda Charitra Nātakam the comparison is only an extension of such superficial observation of similarities between the two traditions. But a more meticulous analysis of the two traditions, both at the level of a study of the repertoires and at the level of the details of a particular item taken up in the present study, brings to light interesting aspects of contrast between the twin traditions.

Though Prahlāda Charitra Nātakam has been chosen for the present work because of its significance in both the traditions, the other common items between Kūchipūdi and Mélattūr, like Ushāparinayam, etc., may provide better insights for a fruitful comparative study of the two traditions. Since Ushāparinayam has no ritualistic association, a comparative study of this dance drama in Kūchipūdi and Mélattūr traditions may reveal certain new aspects of artistic orientation in Mélattūr tradition.

The author is aware of the Mélattūr Bhāgavata Méla Nātakam type of performances, especially of Prahlāda Charitra Nātakam, found in different villages like Ootukkādu, Sālaimangalam, Sūlamangalam, and Téperumanallūr – the neighbouring villages of Mélattūr. For the convenience of focus these performances have been set aside in the present research work. The Mélattūr Prahlāda Charitra Nātakam performance has been taken as the most representative of all these Prahlāda Charitra Nātakam performances.

In fact, apart from the Mélattūr tradition there are many other cognate traditions to Kūchipūdi. One good example is the Tūrpu Bhāgavatam tradition of the Eastern Andhra Pradesh, and even Kathākali of Kerala has the commonness of being a dance-drama tradition. A comparative study of Kūchipūdi and these other South Indian Dance-drama traditions may also be fruitful in unearthing many hitherto unexplored aspects of these traditions.

It is interesting to note that Prahlāda Charitra Nātakam is also prevalent in the Ganjam District of South Orissa and the Terukkūtu tradition of Tamil Nadu. There are many striking parallels between the Kūchipūdi and Mélattūr Prahlāda Charitra Nātakams on the one hand, and these Prahlāda Charitra Nātakams on the other. An interesting aspect of the comparability of these traditions is that the Prahlāda Charitra Nātakam of Ganjam District of South Orissa is geographically close to the area of Tūrpu Bhāgavatam tradition. Similarly, the Terukkūtu tradition belongs to the state of Tamil Nadu as does the Mélattūr tradition. A comparative study of all these Prahlāda Charitra Nātakams may be an immensely fruitful exercise.

Kūchipūdi tradition, because of its wide repertoire, shares such comparability with many other Indian classical dance traditions. For example, the identity of Kūchipūdi with Bhāmākalapam item is also found in Tūrpu Bhāgavatam and Andhra Nātyam traditions. A comparative study of Bhāmākalapam in all these three forms can also be taken up. The Ashtapadis of the Kūchipūdi tradition have their parallels in Odissi and many other North Indian dance traditions. Kshétrayya Padams are found in

Bharatanātyam and Andhra Nātyam traditions. Even Sabdams are common between Kūchipūdi and Bharatanātyam.

All these similarities the Kūchipūdi tradition shares with the other dance traditions, when probed, may reveal several interesting, hitherto unobserved, aspects. Such a comparative study of the Kūchipūdi tradition with various other Indian Classical Dance traditions is a gigantic task that needs collaboration of many researchers.

The research on which the book has been based reveals the artistic priority in the Kūchipūdi tradition over the ritualistic aspect, and the impact of that priority today is observed on different aspects, like amazingly wide repertoire, nature of music compositions, choreography, body movements, rhythmic compositions, etc. These revelations may help in grasping several intricate aspects of Kūchipūdi tradition, like the scope for change, adaptation, innovation, invention and transformation within the limitations of its identity and traditional characteristics.

Bibliography

ENGLISH

Acharya, C.R. 1965. *Kuchipudi and Ritual Dances of Andhra Pradesh. Sangeetha Natya Kala Sangraham,* Bombay,

Acharya, C.R. and Mallika Sarabhai. 1992. *Understanding Kuchipudi.* New Delhi.

Anuradha, J., 1993. *Kuchipudi Dance - Who is who.* Bombay.

Appa Rao, Vissa. 1954. *Kuchipudi: Indian Dance.* New Delhi.

App Rao, Vissa. 1959. 'Dance Art in Andhra Pradesh'. *Souvenir on Kuchipudi Natya Seminar.* Hyderabad.

Appa Rao, Vissa. 1959. 'Kuchipudi School of Dancing'. *Souvenir on Kuchipudi Natya Seminar.* Hyderabad.

Arudra. 1986. 'The Mēlattūr Mela: The Telugu Heritage of Tamilnadu'. *Sruti* 2 (April).

Arudra. 1989. 'Background and Evolution of Kuchipudi Dance'. *Sruti* 54 (March).

Arudra. 1994. 'Lingaring Questions: Some Fashionable Fallacies', *Sruti* 115 (April).

Arudra. 1995. 'Kuchipudi-The Abode of Dance'. *Andhra Jagati.* Madras.

Ashton & Christie. 1977. *Yaksagana: A dance-drama of India.* New Delhi.

Balakrishnan, Shyamala. 1981. 'Therukoothu: The Folk Theatre of Tamilnadu. *Vivekananda Patrika*, (August).

Chinna Satyam, Vempati. 1985. 'The Roots of Kuchipudi Art'. *Sangeeta Natya Kala Sangraham*. Bombay,

Ghosh, M.M. (trans). 1957. *Nandikeswara's Abhinaya Darpana,* Calcutta, (first published in 1934).

Ghosh, M.M. 1930. *Natya Sastra.* Calcutta.

Khokar, Mohan. 1981. 'The Renaissance of Indian Dance and its Consequences'. *Vivekanda Patrika* (August), (Source Bhavan's Journal, August 5, 1962).

Khokar, Mohan. 1993. 'Kuchipudi: Must women Dance Solo? Degeneration, Not Development'. *The illustrated Weekly of India* (20th March).

Kothari, Sunil. 1977. 'The Dance Drama tradition of Kuchipudi, Bhagavata Mela Nataka and Kuravanji with special reference to Rasa theory as expounded in Bhāratas Natya Sastra'. *Ph.D Thesis submitted to M.S. University Baroda.*

Naidu, M.A. 1975. *Kuchipudi Classical Dance.* Hyderabad.

Narasimhacharya, Madabhushini. 1989. *History of the Cult of Narasimha in Telangana.* Hyderabad: Sri Malola Grantha Mala, Sri Ahobila Math.

Narasimhacharya, Madabhushini. 1989. *History of the Cult of Narasimha in Telangana.* Hyderabad: Published by Sri Malola Grantha Mala, Sri Ahobila Math.

Natrajan, S. 1990. 'Bhagavata Mela Nataka Tradition and its history at Mélattūr'. *SLNJBMNNS Golden Jubilee Souvenir: 90,* Mélattūr,

Natrajan, S. 1990. 'Bhagavatamela Now and Then'. *SLNJBMNNS Golden Jubilee Souvenir: 90,* Mélattūr,

Partha Sarathi, T.S. 1990. 'Bhārata Natyam and Allied Dances of South India.' *SLNJBMNNS Golden Jubilee Souvenir: 90,* Mélattūr,

Parthasarathi, R.M.L. 1995. 'The Unique Features of Melattur Bhagavata Mela tradition'. *Bhagavata Mela Natya Natakam Souvenir,* Mélattūr.

Patanjali, V. 1981. 'Kuchipudi Dance'. *Vivekananda Patrika*, (August), (Source: Swarajya Nov: 1979).

Patnaik, D.N. 1992. 'Prahlad Natak'. *Sangeeth Natak* 104 (April-June).

Pattabhi Raman, N. 1989. 'Dr. Vempati China Satyam-Modernizer of a Tacky Dance Traditions'. *Sruti* 50/52 (December 1988 - Jan 1989).

Raghavan, V. 1981. 'The Veedhi Bhagavatam of Andhra'. *Vivekananda Patrika* (August).

Ragini Devi. 1966. 'The Revival of Kuchipudi Nritya'. *Marg XIX* : 2 (March).

Ramanan, K.V. 1981. 'Temples as patrons of Dance'. *Vivekananda Patrika* (August).

Ranga Rao, V.A.K. 1984. 'On choreography and Sanchari Bhava', *Sruti* 54 (March).

Ranga Rao, V.A.K. 1989. 'The Transformation of Kuchipudi Dance - The Doctor's perceptions of performance'. *Sruti* 51/52 (Dec 1988 - Jan 1989).

Seetha, S. 1981. *Tanjore as a seat of music.* Madras: University of Madras.

Srinivasan, P. 1982. 'The music in Kuchipudi operas'. *The Journal of Music Academy: XII,* Madras.

Subhadra Murty, K. 1994. 'Siddendhra Yogi Kalakshetra in Kuchipudi'. *Sruti* 115 (APRIL).

Sundara Rajan, V.S. 1990. 'Golden Jubilee of Bhagavata Mela Sangam celebrations Mēlattūr'. *Sruti* 70 (August).

Sundaram, B.M. 1994. 'Bhagavata Mela staged in three villages, differences in approach'. *Sruti* 118 (July).

Surya Prakasha Rao, Kotcheriakota. 1993. 'Kuchipudi Dance music - Some Reminiscences'. *Sovenir of Kuchipudi Mahotsav: 93.* Bombay.

Tandava Krishna, Ayyanki. 1956. 'Kuchipudi Dance'. *Andhra Pradesh Souvenir.* New Delhi.

Vaidhyanatham, Saroja. 1978. *The science of Bhāratanatyam.* New Delhi, 1984.

Varadpande, M.L., *Tradition of Indian Theatre.* New Delhi.

Vasudev, S.V. 1982. 'What's Kuchipudi'. *The Illustrated Weekly of India.* (25th December).

Vatsyayan, Kapila. 1974. *Indian Classical Dance.* New Delhi: Publications Division

Vatsyayan, Kapila. 1980. *Traditional Indian Theatre - multiple streams.* New Delhi.

Vatsyayan, Kapila. 1985. *Traditions of Indian Folk Dance.* New Delhi.

Venugopala Rao, Pappu. 1994. 'Kuchipudi During 1983-93 - Trend Towards solo items'. *Sruti* 115 (APRIL).

Venugopala Rao, Pappu. 1995. 'Kuchipudi'. *Sruti* 135 (December).

TELUGU

Acharya, C.R. 1969. *Kuchipudi Aradhana Nrityamulu.* Eluru.

Andhra University Series:

Yakshaganamulu (Tanjavuru) No: *55.* Waltair, 1955.

Yakshaganamulu (Tanjavuru) No: *56.* Waltair, 1956.

Yakshaganamulu (Tanjavuru) No: *66.* Waltair, 1959.

Yakshaganamulu (Tanjavuru) No: *67.* Waltair, 1960.

Yakshaganamulu (Tanjavuru) No: *72.* Waltair, 1964.

Appa Rao, P.S.R., Rama Rao, Uma. 1994. *Kuchipudi Nrityam.* Hyderabad.

Bhujangaraya Sarma, S.V. 1986. *Kuchipudi Nritya Rupakamulu.* Madras.

Joga Rao, S.V. 1955. *The Kalapam. Triveni* (January).

Joga Rao, S.V. 1955. *Yaksagdnamulu: Sampradayika Patralu. Kinnera* (January).

Joga Rao, S.V. 1961. *Andhra Yakshagana Vangamaya Charitra.* Waltair: Andhra University Publications.

Kanakalingeswara Rao, Banda. 1963. *Kuchipudi Nrityam.* Souvenir on the Golden Jubilee of Dr. Neelam Sanjeeva Reddy, Hyderabad.

Krishnamurthy, Salva and Mutnuri Sangamesam, 1993. *Bhāmā Kalāpam of Kuchipudi. Souvenir of Kuchipuḍi Mahatsav, 93.* Bombay.

Lakshminarasimha Sastry, Chintalapati. 1981. *Kuchipudi Bhagavatulu.* Tenali

Parvatisam, Vedantam. 1952. *Bhagavatulu Kuchipudi.* Vijayawada.

Parvatisam, Vedantam. 1964. *Kuchipudi Vari Bhāmākalapam.* Machilipatanam.

Parvatisam, Vedantam. 1970. *Kuchipudi Pagativeshamulu. Natyakala.*

Parvatisam, Vedantam. 1981. *Kuchipudi Prahlada Natakamu.* Kuchipudi: Own Publication.

Parvatisam, Vedantam. 1988. *Nritya Tarangini.* Vijayawada.

Parvatisam, Vedantam. 1990. *Kuchipudi Melakartalu.* Vijayawada.

Radhakrisna Murthy, Mikkilineni. 1992. *Teluguvari Janapada Kalarupalu.* Hyderabad.

Ramakrishna, Natraj. 1968. *Daksindtya Natyakala Charitra.* Vijayawada.

Ramakrishna, Natraj. 1987. *Andhra Natyam-Kuchipudi.* Hyderabad.

Ramanadham, Chinta. 1974. *Kuchipudi Kala Sagaramu.* Kuchipudi.

Ramanadham, Chinta. 1988. *Kuchipudi Natya Bharati.* Kuchipudi.

Ramanadham, Chinta. 1988. *Kuchipudi Natyacharyulu Charitra Putalu.* Kuchipudi.

List of Eminent Scholars/Exponents/Artists Interviewed

1. Padmasri Nataraj Ramakrishna, Hyderabad.
2. Padmasri Vedantam Satyanarayana Saram, Kūchipūdi.
3. Late Sri. Vedantam Rattayya Sarma, Lecturer, Siddhendra Kalakshetram, Kūchipūdi.
4. Late Sri. Chinta Ramanadham, Principal, Siddhendra Kalakshetram, Kūchipūdi.

5. Late Sri, Vendantam Parvatisam, Kūchipūdi.
6. Sri. P.V.G. Krishna Sarma, Kūchipūdi.
7. Sri. Vedantam Radhesyam, Lecturer Siddhendra Kalakshetram, Kūchipūdi.
8. Sri. Pasumarti Sitaramayya, Kūchipūdi exponent Andhra University, Visakhapatnam.
9. Late Sri. Hemadri Chidambara Dikshitulu, Kūchipūdi exponent Rajahmundry.
10. Late Sri. Chintalapati Varahala Raju, Musicologist, Chodavaram.
11. Late Sri. C. Rama Murthy, Bhārata Natyam exponent, Vizianagaram.
12. Late Sri. Tampallela Suryanarayana, Musicologist, Hyderabad.
13. Late Dr. Arudṛa, Madras.
14. Sri. Gopala Krishna Sarma, Mélattūr.
15. Sri. S. Natarajan, Bhagavata Mela exponent, Mélattūr.
16. Sri. S. Kumar, Bhagavata Mela exponent, Mélattūr.
17. Sri. R. Partha Sarathy, Scholar, Kumbhakonam.
18. Sri. Srikantha and Vijay, Madras.
19. Prof. Madurai Mani, New Delhi.

Index